Homer's
Iliad

Edited & with
an Introduction
by Harold Bloom

© 2000 by Chelsea House Publishers, a division of Main Line Book Co.

Introduction © 1996 by Harold Bloom

All rights reserved. No part of this publication may be reproduced or transmitted in any form or by any means without the written permission of the publisher.

Printed and bound in the United States of America.

First Printing
1 3 5 7 9 8 6 4 2

ISBN: 0-7910-4130-1

Chelsea House Publishers
1974 Sproul Road, Suite 400
P.O. Box 914
Broomall, PA 19008-0914

The Chelsea House World Wide Web site address is
http://www.chelseahouse.com

Contents

Editor's Note	4
Introduction	5
Biography of Homer	7
Thematic and Structural Analysis	11
List of Characters	30
Critical Views	
Dionysius of Halicarnassus: Homer's Skill at Word-Painting	33
Alexander Pope: Homer's Imagination	34
John Addington Symonds: The Structural and Thematic Integrity of the *Iliad*	36
John A. Scott: The Wrath of Achilles	39
C. M. Bowra: The Heroic in Homer	40
Rachel Bespaloff: Helen	45
H. T. Wade-Gery: The Historical Basis of the *Iliad*	47
Cedric H. Whitman: The Structure of the *Iliad*	50
Denys L. Page: The Origins of the *Iliad*	53
André Michalopoulos: Heroic Elements in the *Iliad*	55
Charles Rowan Beye: The Looseness of Structure of the *Iliad*	58
W. F. Jackson Knight: The Appeal of Homer's Epic Poetry	60
James M. Redfield: Hector and Achilles	62
William G. Thalmann: The Death of Achilles and the Epic Cycle	64
Paolo Vivante: Hector's Character	67
M. M. Willcock: Idomeneus	69
Mark W. Edwards: Ancient Greek Folktales and the *Iliad*	72
Katherine Callan King: Common Motifs in the *Iliad*	76
Keith Stanley: The Significance of the *Iliad*	78
Graham Zanker: Achilles and Priam	80
Works by Homer	84
Works about Homer and *The Iliad*	86
Index of Themes and Ideas	90

Editor's Note

My Introduction explores the otherness of Achilles in regard to us, which paradoxically now enhances his aesthetic value for us. The poet-translator Alexander Pope's praise of Homer's inventiveness is followed by J. A. Symonds arguing for the unity of the *Iliad* and by John A. Scott on Homer's canonical legacy.

C. M. Bowra contrasts heroism in the *Iliad* to later Western manifestations, while Rachel Bespaloff gives us an appreciation of the peerless Helen of Troy. The poem's status as fiction, not history, is stressed by H. T. Wade-Gery, after which C. H. Whitman proposes a theory of the poem's structure. Oral tradition is emphasized by Denys L. Page, while André Michalopoulos adumbrates the heroism of Achilles, and Charles Rowan Beye finds the poem's disjointed structure to be a product of oral tradition. The pleasures of the *Iliad* are highlighted by W. F. Jackson Knight, after which James M. Redfield contrasts Achilles and Hestor, and W. G. Thalmann concentrates upon the death of Achilles.

Paolo Vivante expounds Hector's character, while M. M. Willcock considers Idomeneus, and Mark W. Edwards comments upon Homer's use of folk material. Achilles' status as "best of the Achaians" is examined by Katherine Callan King, after which Keith Stanley further illuminates the *Iliad*'s relation to oral tradition.

In the final extract, Graham Zanker comments upon the poignant scene between Achilles and Priam, which is one of the great achievements of Homer's art.

Introduction

HAROLD BLOOM

Together with the Bible, the *Iliad* represents the foundation of Western literature, thought, and spirituality: of culture in the broadest sense. That banal truism contains the permanent split in Western consciousness: Our cognition and aesthetics are Greek, but our religion and morality—whether Christian, Moslem, Judaic—make us people of the Book, and the book is not the *Iliad*, as it was for classical culture. We are at once very close to the *Iliad*, even when we first encounter it, and enormously estranged from it. The largest of Simone Weil's many eccentricities came when she closely associated the Gospels and the *Iliad*, while opposing to them the Hebrew Bible and Roman literature. Jesus and Achilles do not pair at all easily, and the morality of the *Iliad* is totally antithetical to that of the New Testament. This division in Western consciousness never has been healed, even by Shakespeare, whose Hamlet is far closer to King David than to Achilles or to Hector, and whose Lear sustains comparison with the Solomon of Ecclesiastes and the apocryphal Wisdom of Solomon much more readily than with Priam, or with Peleus, the wretched father of Achilles. The *Iliad* was the schoolbook of Athens, and we, all of us, are still attending the school of Athens, but we are there as aliens, barbarians not wholly at one with the thought-forms and aesthetic shapes that necessarily we must absorb if we are to be coherent beings.

The *Iliad* centers upon telling us that the highest good is victory, explicitly in war, implicitly in art and thought: indeed in every human endeavor. Homer teaches *agon*, the contest for the foremost place, a teaching we ourselves honor more readily in politics or in sport or in business or in law, than we do in the arts and in the other realms of the intellect and the spirit. Achilles, best of the Greeks, is the epitome of the agonistic. His language, as Adam Parry observed, is "a form of action," and yet he is able to hint his disillusionment with his own glory, and with nature, for denying him literal immortality. Adam Parry remarks that Achilles "asks questions that cannot be answered and makes demands that cannot be met." Homer's complexity contains Achilles' extraordinary dilemma: The hero has wearied of the *agon,* and no longer desires its spoils, but he cannot abandon a society that knows no value except the agonistic ones, and he has no language beyond that of *agon.* Hamlet, radically alienated from Elsinore, has infinite resources of language in which to exploit that alienation, even though Hamlet also has abandoned all faith in language or in the self, his own included. The epic plangency of Achilles is that he turns again to action as his form of language, and paradoxically kills out of his very hatred for mortality, including his own mortality.

The heroes of the Hebrew Bible—Abraham, Jacob, Joseph, David—have no affinities whatsoever with Achilles. Even David, the only professional warrior among them, carries on their blessing from Yahweh and so is in a position beyond tragedy, despite his many griefs that terminate in the death of his beloved son, Absalom. You can make a covenant with Yahweh and then trust in the covenant, but no one can trust Zeus. Achilles is half a god, and he says that "who trusts himself to the gods will gain their hearing," but he knows that the response to such a hearing is likely to be equivocal. And what can the gods do for him anyway? They cannot make him physically immortal, and they cannot free him from war, since despite his disillusion he *is* war and nothing but war. The poetic strength of Achilles is that he is a force or a drive, even though he feels, thinks, and perceives as a man. No other purely literary figure is nearly as heroic, or as aesthetically satisfying to us, but Achilles' *otherness,* in relation to us, is now his dominant characteristic. ✤

Biography of Homer

Homer (Homeros) is the reputed author of the two oldest epic poems of ancient Greece, the *Iliad* and the *Odyssey*. Even the Greeks, however, were uncertain of the very existence of Homer or of the time in which he lived, and it is now believed that, if there actually was a Homer, he did no more than organize or edit the poems roughly in the form in which they have come down to us.

In the 1930s Milman Parry discovered that the Homeric poems belonged to the tradition of oral poetry, in which long passages were committed to memory by bards or "rhapsodes" and recited in public assemblies or at the courts of kings or chieftains. Some parts of the Homeric poems—especially the *Iliad*, which is thought to be older than the *Odyssey*—probably predate the Trojan War (traditionally dated to 1184 B.C.E. but now dated by archaeological evidence to roughly 1220 B.C.E.). Conversely, other parts of the poems must date to a much later period. Homer probably brought the various sections of the two poems together no later than 700 B.C.E. All the works attributed to Homer are in an archaic form of the Ionic dialect of Greek, mostly spoken in what is now western Turkey.

Seven cities in Greece, both on the mainland and on some of the islands in the Aegean Sea, claimed the honor of being the birthplace of Homer. The conventional belief that he was blind rests largely upon a passage in the so-called *Homeric Hymns*, a series of thirty-three poems celebrating the gods of the Greek pantheon. Many rhapsodes, however, were in fact blind.

The *Iliad* and the *Odyssey* are each unified in themselves, although they are very different from each other in tone and subject matter. The *Iliad* deals with the final stages of the Trojan War between the Greeks and the Trojans, and most of the action takes place in the Troad (a region in northwestern Turkey). The ostensible cause of the war is the abduction of Helen (the wife of Menelaus) by Paris; but the *Iliad* focuses largely on the personal battle between the Greek Achilles and the Trojan Hector. Although much of the poem is taken up with battles, there is a lofty, aristocratic character to the *Iliad* that may reflect the attitudes of the nobility prior to the classical age of Greek civilization. The poem is resolved when Achilles defeats Hector in single combat and, after dragging his body around the walls of Troy in triumph, hands it over to Hector's father Priam.

The events in the *Iliad* are not, of course, likely to be a literal account of a historical event. Although there probably was something corresponding to the Trojan War, it now seems clear that the war was waged not between two groups of racially or ethnically distinct peoples (Greeks and Trojans) but between two factions of early Greeks, called Mycenaeans, who flourished in the second millennium B.C.E. The cause of the war may have been a dispute over the control of the Hellespont, the narrow channel leading to the Black Sea.

It is believed by many that the *Odyssey* was assembled at a much later date than the *Iliad,* since it seems to reflect a greater knowledge of the Mediterranean world as gained by the Greeks in their colonizing and trading ventures in the ninth and eighth centuries B.C.E. The *Odyssey* is an adventure story about the wanderings of Odysseus after the Trojan War. His travels take him as far west as the islands of the Hesperides (perhaps a reference to Gibraltar) and even to the Greek underworld, where he meets the souls of the dead. Eventually Odysseus returns home to the small island of Ithaca (off the western coast of Greece), defeats the suitors who have been vainly courting his wife, Penelope, for twenty years, and reunites with her and with his son, Telemachus.

Several other works were attributed by the Greeks either to Homer or to the *Homeridae* ("the sons of Homer"). These include the Trojan Cycle (a group of six epic poems—most now surviving only in fragments—dealing with other aspects of the Trojan War than were covered by Homer), the *Homeric Hymns,* and three burlesques or parodies: the *Margites;* the *Cercopes* ("Monkey-Men"); and the *Batrachomyomachia* ("Battle of the Frogs and Mice"). The first two of these parodies exist only in brief fragments. All these poems were written considerably later than the *Iliad* and *Odyssey,* dating from the seventh to the fifth centuries B.C.E.

The Homeric poems were, in essence, the Bible of the Greeks. They incorporated much of what was believed about the gods (Zeus, Hera, Athena, Apollo, Hermes, and many others), who were thought to dwell on the top of Mount Olympus in northeastern Greece. Although Homer was an immense influence on subsequent Greek literature, the esteem in which he and his work were held is reflected by the fact that no later poet in Greece or Rome ever retold the stories of Achilles and Hector or of Odysseus, even though most of the other legends about the Greek gods and heroes were retold many times by poets, dramatists, and historians.

The *Iliad* and the *Odyssey* were each divided into twenty-four books in the third century B.C.E. At this time the Greeks began to lay the groundwork for later scholarship and criticism by determining the proper text of the poems (certain portions were deemed spurious or the work of later interpolators) and by writing commentaries elucidating the poems. An important commentary was written by the scholar Aristarchus (c. 216–c. 144 B.C.E.), large fragments of which survive.

Homer was tremendously influential on Latin literature as well. His greatest disciple was Vergil (P. Vergilius Maro), who toward the end of the first century B.C.E. wrote the *Aeneid,* an epic poem consciously based upon the *Iliad* and the *Odyssey* telling the tale of the wanderings of Aeneas (a minor figure mentioned in the *Iliad*) from Troy to Italy. The Romans referred to Odysseus as Ulixes or Ulysses.

The influence of the Homeric poems upon Western literature has been incalculable; it can be sensed from works as diverse as Dante's *Divine Comedy* and James Joyce's *Ulysses* (1922). The modern Greek poet Nikos Kazantzakis wrote a sequel to the *Odyssey* under the title *Odysseia* (1938; translated into English in 1958 as *The Odyssey: A Modern Sequel*).

Homer's works were among the earliest to be published when printing was invented in the mid-fifteenth century. The work of many scholars has now established the Greek text of

Homer on as sound a basis as possible, and many helpful commentaries have been written, notably an exhaustive commentary on the *Iliad* by G. S. Kirk (1985–93).

The *Iliad* was first translated into English by the poet George Chapman in 1611. Since then, many distinguished writers have published translations of both the Homeric poems, from Thomas Hobbes to Alexander Pope to William Cullen Bryant to Robert Fagles. Some of these translations have been in prose, including one by Andrew Lang, Walter Leaf, and Ernest Myers, and another by Samuel Butler. The translation of the *Iliad* by the classical scholar Richmond Lattimore attempts a line-for-line translation and perhaps captures the flavor of the Greek original better than many others. ✣

Thematic and Structural Analysis

The mythic cause of the Trojan War was the crime of the Trojan prince Paris, who, while visiting Menelaus, a king of the Achaians, met and ran off with his host's wife, Helen. But this abduction was instigated by a divine conflict: the contest among the Olympian goddesses Hera, Athena, and Aphrodite over who was most beautiful. Paris had been selected to judge them, and he chose Aphrodite, in exchange for which she "gave" him Helen, her counterpart in beauty among mortals. His subsequent "theft"—monumental in a culture built upon honor and the sacred protocol between guests and hosts—drove the Achaians (led by Menelaus' brother, Agamemnon) to wage war upon the Trojans (led by Paris' brother, Hector). When the *Iliad* begins, the war is in its tenth year and the gods themselves are divided over its outcome. But the epic presents the initial conflict in microcosm, recounting the course of the war after the abduction of yet another woman. This time the crime occurs within the Achaian ranks, the perpetrator is Agamemnon, and the man wronged is Achilles, "the best of all the Achaians" fighting for Menelaus. Thus although the epic encompasses international and divine conflict, it focuses, as the first line announces, upon the anger of Achilles.

Book one opens when Agamemnon, as part of his war spoils, has taken a young woman, Chryseis, as mistress. Her father, however, is a priest of Apollo, and he calls upon the god to intercede for her return; Apollo attacks the Achaians for nine days (mirroring in miniature the nine years of war). When Achilles asks Kalchas, the augur, why Apollo is angry, he nervously explains and adds that the god will continue his onslaught until Chryseis is returned. But Agamemnon says he will give her up only if he can have Achilles' own mistress, Briseis. At this Achilles explodes, his anger compounded by the nine years he and his men have spent fighting the Trojans for Agamemnon and Menelaus' honor, and he says that he will withdraw. Nestor, respected for his age and wisdom, tries to persuade the two to compromise, but Agamemnon insists that he is king, while Achilles, for his part, can claim to be the

Achaians' champion as well as the son of the goddess Thetis. The two part enraged.

Later, however, Agamemnon does release Chryseis—but in retaliation he orders Briseis to be taken from Achilles. Though the hero is incensed, he does not keep Agamemnon's men from carrying out their orders, and Briseis is taken away "all unwilling." Later Achilles weeps and calls to his goddess mother, Thetis, who rises from the sea to attend her son. Achilles laments that he was born "to be a man with a short life" yet is not even granted honor. He asks her to convince the gods to turn the war against the Achaians so that "wide-ruling Agamemnon may recognize / his madness, that he did no honour to the best of the Achaians." Thetis promises to persuade Zeus.

In the meantime, Chryseis is returned to her father, and sacrifices are made to Apollo, who ends his siege upon the Achaians. But on Olympus, Thetis entreats Zeus to let the Trojans overpower the Achaians for a while, and Zeus promises to consider the matter. He warns his jealous wife, Hera, who bitterly hates the Trojans (Paris especially for judging Aphrodite more beautiful than herself), not to interfere when she suspects Thetis' machinations. Thus, as book one ends, Achilles' anger, spurred by the abduction of a woman, has split the Achaian forces and further divided the gods.

Zeus then sends Dream to tell Agamemnon that if he attacks the Trojans he will win (**book two**). Dream appears to Agamemnon in the likeness of Nestor, so he believes the message—"fool, who [knows] nothing of all the things Zeus planned." Agamemnon assembles the reluctant Achaians, who, after much dissent, are finally impelled by the threat of disgrace and the promise of victory to follow their king. At this point, Homer lists the Achaian chiefs in the famous "catalogue of ships," detailing the warriors' origins, homelands, and abilities; this may seem a dry recitation but in fact provides fascinating (although disputed) information on the relative political, social, and military conditions of the places cited. But, among the thousands of famed chiefs, far best of all is Achilles, who stays "apart among his curved sea-wandering vessels, / raging at Agamemnon."

In the meantime, the "wind-footed" goddess Iris speeds to the Trojans with word that the Achaians plan an attack, and Hector—son of King Priam and leader of the Trojans—calls his soldiers to arms. Book two ends with a list of those in the Trojan camp, mirroring the catalogue of ships.

The two sides then advance, the Trojans "with clamour and shouting," and the Achaians "silently, breathing valour" (**book three**). Paris leaps forward from the Trojan ranks, but "his cheeks [are] seized with a green pallor" when he faces Menelaus. Hector, who has been forced to lead the Trojans in this war on behalf of his brother, steps in to rebuke him: "Evil Paris, beautiful, woman-crazy, cajoling, / better had you never been born, or killed unwed." Paris then suggests that both sides lay down their arms while he fight Menelaus singly "for the sake of Helen and all her possessions." Menelaus agrees, and he bids the Achaians make a sacrifice for victory.

Meanwhile Iris goes to Helen's chamber, where she is "weaving a great web, / a red folding robe, and working into it the numerous struggles / of Trojans, breakers of horses, and bronze-armoured Achaians." Although weaving is a typical occupation for a woman in this culture, it is often invested in Homeric and later literature with a symbolic significance, suggesting women's alleged ensnaring qualities. Iris tells Helen of the pending battle, which leaves in her heart "sweet longing after her husband of time before." She goes to the ramparts to observe the fight but is herself seen by the Trojan elders, who say, "Surely there is no blame on Trojans and strong-greaved Achaians / if for long time they suffer hardship for a woman like this one."

After the appropriate sacrifices are made, Paris and Menelaus arm themselves and stride forward. Calling on Zeus "to punish the man who first did . . . injury," Menelaus hurls his spear, lightly wounding Paris. Paris' helmet strap becomes caught at his chin and Menelaus has nearly dragged him away before Aphrodite intervenes, breaking the strap. She then wraps Paris in a mist, sets him in his own perfumed bedchamber, and hurries to fetch Helen. Although Helen refuses to go to Paris as "it would be too shameful," Aphrodite forces her. When Helen sees Paris she half-jeeringly advises him not to fight again. But he responds that he may have lost this battle but will win the next, as there are gods on the Trojans' side too. Paris draws Helen into bed, while on the battlefield Agamemnon declares Menelaus the victor and orders Helen and her possessions returned.

The gods then assemble, and Zeus suggests that the war be ended and Troy allowed to stand (**book four**). Hera and Athena are enraged by the idea, which would "make wasted and fruitless" the nine years of fighting, and urge that the war go on. Zeus consents, sending Athena "to make it so that the Trojans are first offenders" against the truce.

Athena descends to incite the Trojan Pandaros to break the peace by shooting Menelaus. But she herself protects Menelaus, brushing the arrow away from his skin so he is only grazed. Seeing his brother's wound, Agamemnon shudders and swears that Troy will perish. As Menelaus is tended with healing drugs, the Trojans attack again, and Agamemnon rallies his fighters against the Trojan "liars." Agamemnon's role as king and the righteous unity of the Achaians are emphasized, while the Trojans by contrast must issue battle cries in many languages because they have been "called from many far places." In the battle that follows—the first of many—countless warriors' grisly deaths are detailed.

As the fighting continues (**book five**), the gods themselves take part: The guileful Athena even leads "manslaughtering, blood-stained" Ares, the god of war, out of the battle so he cannot help the Trojans and then herself returns to help the Achaians. When the Trojan hero Aeneas, son of Aphrodite, is struck, Aphrodite shields him with her white robe but then is herself speared through the hand by the Achaian Diomedes. Shrieking, she drops her son, whom Apollo catches. The gods temporarily withdraw, but not for long as Ares soon returns to drive the Trojans on, which again incites Athena and Hera to join the battle until Athena herself helps Diomedes drive a spear into Ares' belly. The wounded Ares goes to Zeus to complain, and Zeus, calling him "the most hateful of all gods," nevertheless has him healed. Hera and Athena return to Olympus, content that they have stopped Ares.

When the two sides are left on their own, the Trojans are chased back and are about to retreat inside their walls when the augur Helenos, Hector's brother, rouses them (**book six**). He urges Hector to have their mother assemble the women to sacrifice to Athena so she will protect them from Diomedes. In a memorable scene suggesting the complexities and ambiguities of this war, Diomedes is about to attack the Trojan Glaukos but is struck by his bravery and asks him who he is. Identifying themselves with elaborate stories, the two heroes recognize each other, drop their spears, and exchange vows of friendship.

By now, Hector has entered the palace and bids his mother, Hekabe, to pray to Athena. He then finds Paris with Helen in his bedchamber and admonishes him to fight. Helen, calling herself "a nasty bitch evil-intriguing," asks Hector to rest a while, but he wants to see his own wife (Andromache) and son because, he says, "I do not know if ever again I shall come back this way." When Andromache sees him, she pleads tearfully for him to stay. But Hector refuses: "[M]ay I be dead and the piled earth hide me under before I / hear you crying and know by this that they drag you captive." He bids his family farewell, and, in one of the epic's most effective scenes, must laughingly remove his helmet before embracing his small boy, who screams to see his father's face within "the bronze and the crest with its horse-hair." Paris catches up with Hector, and they return to the battle.

Their energetic fighting encourages the Trojans (**book seven**). Athena, seeing the two destroying the Achaians, speeds back to Troy, where she meets Apollo, who is just as intent on defending the Trojans. The two agree to postpone the fighting for the day and to have Hector challenge the Achaians to single combat with a chosen champion. Helenos divines their wishes and easily persuades Hector, who makes the challenge to the Achaians. But they are "stricken to silence / in shame of refusing him, and in fear to take up his challenge," until Menelaus angrily offers to fight—although greatly outmatched. Agamemnon stops him, saying that even Achilles "trembles to meet this man." When Nestor scolds the reluctant Achaians, several finally rise, and Agamemnon draws lots among them. Aias, son of Telemon, wins.

The Achaians pray to Zeus for Aias and rejoice when they see him armed, "smiling under his threatening brows" and "shaking the spear far-shadowing." He and Hector then go "at each other like lions who live on raw meat," each hurling his spear and striking but not wounding the other. They fight hand to hand, and Aias lightly wounds Hector in the neck. But as the Trojan is falling back, Apollo lifts him, and heralds separate the two fighters, saying that both are beloved of Zeus, and as it is night they must stop fighting—and the scene is again emblematic of the taut balance of the war.

After this confrontation, Agamemnon sacrifices an ox to Zeus, the Achaians feast, and Nestor proposes a temporary truce so that they may bury their dead. The Trojans, meanwhile, are angry at this endless bloodshed, and the counselor Antenor suggests that they give up Helen. But Paris says he will return all the possessions he took from Menelaus but "will not give back the woman." Priam, like Nestor, proposes a brief truce, and the next day the Trojans present Paris' offer to the Achaians. It is refused, but the two sides agree to spend the day tending to their dead. The Achaians also build a wall of defense, which angers Poseidon, who, with Apollo, had built Troy's original walls; Zeus agrees to let Poseidon "break the wall to pieces and scatter it into the salt sea" once the Achaians have destroyed Troy—an example of the gods', or the narrator's, omniscient foretelling. As the Achaians feast, Zeus thunders all night.

At dawn Zeus assembles the gods on Olympus and warns that none should interfere in the mortals' battle at risk of being dashed "down to the murk of Tartarus" (**book eight**). Athena assures him that they will obey but adds that they will nevertheless "put good counsel in" their favorites. Zeus accepts this and drives off in his chariot to watch the battle.

Zeus keeps tally so that the two sides will be balanced, shifting the advantage from one to the other until finally the Trojans have driven the Achaians back. Seeing this, Hera and Athena are indignant that Zeus has "bent to the wishes of Thetis" in giving honor to Achilles by having the Achaians suffer without him. The goddesses prepare for battle, but Zeus has Iris stop them, threatening to smash their chariot and strike them with lightning. The gods then reunite on Olympus, but Hera and Athena sit apart, muttering and "devising evil for the Trojans" as Zeus reminds them of his strength. He tells them, further, that the next day will see Hector and the Trojans destroy many Achaians and that Hector will not be defeated until Achilles is again forced to battle after his beloved friend Patroklos is killed. As night falls, the unsuspecting Hector tells his armies to rest, light campfires, and prepare for the next day. Although they make sacrifices, "the blessed gods [take] no part of it."

As **book nine** begins, Agamemnon cries out at Zeus' "vile deception" in letting him think the Achaians would win, and Diomedes chides him for his weakness. Nestor advises Agamemnon, who has dishonored a man whom the immortals clearly honor, to make peace with Achilles. Agamemnon admits that he was "mad" and lists the gifts he will offer Achilles: cauldrons, gold, horses, women, even Briseis herself. In return he wants Achilles to yield to him, as he is "kinglier," and to rejoin the battle.

Aias, Odysseus, and Phoinix go to Achilles with the message and find the hero playing the lyre with his beloved friend Patroklos. They make the offer, but Achilles, still angered at his public dishonor in a war in which he has nothing at stake, rejects it. "A man dies still if he has done nothing, as one who has done much," he says, and he reveals that he has two possible destinies: Either he will die fighting the Trojans but earn everlasting glory, or he will return home and live long, but his glory will fade. Having already lost honor, he chooses life. Each of the three messengers tries to persuade him to yield, but Achilles' passion and philosophy are unrelenting. Although the other Achaians are stricken to learn of his refusal, Diomedes declares that Achilles will fight when "the heart in his body urges him to."

That night both sides are restless (**book ten**). Neither Agamemnon nor Menelaus can sleep, so they rise, dress, and wake their chiefs. When all have assembled, Nestor asks for someone to infiltrate the Trojan camp and learn their plans. Diomedes volunteers, selecting Odysseus to accompany him. They arm themselves, and Athena sends a heron, which they do not see but hear crying in the darkness—a good augury.

Both thank the goddess and make their way "like two lions into the black night."

Meanwhile, the sleepless Trojans have also gathered, and Hector has asked who will infiltrate the Achaians' camp. Dolon, "an evil man to look on but . . . swift-footed," volunteers. But he has not gone far before he hears footsteps, and soon Odysseus and Diomedes are upon him. Dolon begs for mercy and, as Odysseus assures him he will not be harmed, tells them which of the Trojans are asleep and where their horses are. Diomedes then strikes him with his sword, and "Dolon's head still speaking [drops] in the dust." Offering his armor to Athena, the two go to the camp of the Trojan allies, the Thracians. There Diomedes kills many sleeping soldiers, while Odysseus unties their horses. Athena warns them to return quickly as Apollo, angered, rouses the Trojans. But Diomedes and Odysseus make it safely back, recount their exploits, bathe, and sacrifice to Athena.

Heavy fighting resumes, with countless men cut down "to no longer delight their wives, but the vultures" (**book eleven**). Zeus protects Hector, sending Iris to warn him to avoid Agamemnon until he has been struck, and then to charge forward. Homer then recounts the many men Agamemnon kills until he is wounded and rides back to the ships. When Hector sees this, he rouses his men and rejoins the fight, and the narrative details his slaughters.

Diomedes and Odysseus are in turn riled by this and stand firm, continuing to kill Trojans. Diomedes throws his spear at Hector and strikes his helmet but does not wound him; he himself is then wounded in the foot by Paris, whom he angrily belittles as an "eyer of young girls" before retreating to the ships. Alone, Odysseus holds his ground as the Trojans pen him in, until finally he is stabbed and the skin is torn away from his ribs, although Athena keeps the spear point from reaching his vitals. When the Trojans see Odysseus wounded, they charge him, he shouts to his companions, and Menelaus and Aias come to his aid. Meanwhile, Hector is killing many at the other end of the battle but returns when he learns of the Achaians' onslaught. Aias, though, continues to advance until Zeus strikes fear into his heart and he is nearly "overpowered by the [Trojans'] dense spears." He fights them off as the Achaians rally to help him.

Meanwhile Achilles, watching from the stern of his ship, sends Patroklos to find out which warrior Nestor has carried off wounded. When Nestor sees Patroklos he begs him to rejoin the fight, even if Achilles himself will not, and suggests that Patroklos wear Achilles' armor to fool the Trojans and boost the Achaians' morale. On his way back to Achilles, Patroklos learns that all "the bravest in battle / are lying up among the ships with arrow or spear wounds." Thus, as the epic approaches its midpoint, the pressure upon Achilles mounts.

The battle rages on, with Hector fighting "like a whirlwind," trying to urge the Trojans over the vast ditch the Achaians have dug to defend themselves (**book twelve**). When their horses refuse, Hector goes ahead on foot, followed by Paris, Helenos, and Aeneas with their men. Zeus protects the Trojans as they battle against the Achaians' defenses, which stand firm.

The two Aiases (sons of Telamon and Oileus) stir up the Achaians while the Trojans—especially Glaukos and Zeus' son Sarpedon—try to penetrate their defenses. The battle is even until Zeus gives "the greater glory to Hector" and lets him smash through the Achaian walls by hurling a huge stone. He bursts in "with a dark face like sudden night, but [shining] with the ghastly / glitter of bronze" and scatters the Achaians.

Now Zeus shifts his attention from Troy, thinking that no immortal will intervene (**book thirteen**). Poseidon, though, pitying the Achaians, strides into the depths of the sea to loose his "flying-footed" horses and go to the Achaians. The Trojans continue their fight behind Hector. But Poseidon, in the guise of Kalchas, speaks to the two Aiases, filling their hearts with daring and making them agile. With their lead, the Achaians form a living wall, linked arm in arm against the Trojans.

The battle is fierce, with Zeus and Poseidon divided against each other. Among the most distinguished Achaians are Idomeneus and his henchman Meriones; among the Trojans, Deiphobos and Aeneas. When a comrade is killed by Idomeneus, Deiphobos summons Aeneas and others, and together they attack, killing the son of Ares. Ares, though, is unaware of this, having left the battle, as Zeus ordered. The slaughter rages on, with Menelaus wounding and killing many. Meanwhile, Hector fights near the Achaians' gates, unaware of the carnage being done elsewhere until Poulydamas counsels him to consolidate. With Paris, Hector goes into the thickest part of the battle. As the Trojans continue to attack the Achaians, Aias taunts Hector, who, enraged, leads the Trojans onward.

Meanwhile Nestor, seeing the onslaught of Trojans and the Achaians' broken wall, goes in search of Agamemnon and finds with him the other wounded Achaian leaders (**book fourteen**). Agamemnon suggests that they all retreat to their ships, but Odysseus, "looking darkly at him," exhorts him to lead, not speak of retreat. Diomedes agrees with Odysseus, and Agamemnon renews his resolve. The scene then shifts to the activities of the gods: Poseidon, disguised as an old man, comes to Agamemnon to spur him on, and Hera, glad to see this, decides to "beguile the brain in Zeus." In her chamber she bathes, anoints her hair and body, and dresses herself in ambrosial robes. She then goes to Aphrodite and, using a false pretense, asks her for a love charm. Aphrodite gives Hera her elaborate zone, or girdle, adorned with "beguilements," "passion of sex," and the "whispered endearment that steals the heart away even from the thoughtful." Then Hera bargains with Sleep to close "the shining eyes of Zeus under his brows / as soon as [she has] lain beside him in love." When Hera goes to Zeus on Mount Ida, he is consumed by passion. Telling her that "never before has love for any goddess or woman / so melted about the heart inside" him, he delivers an extraordinary recitation of those others before finally taking Hera in his arms and wrapping the two in a golden cloud. He then sleeps deeply.

Meanwhile, Sleep tells Poseidon that he has a chance to defend the Achaians. Even though many of the leaders are wounded, they return to the battle with new strength, Poseidon leading and "holding in his heavy hand the stark sword with the thin edge / glittering." The two sides clash again, and Hector attacks Aias but does not wound him. Aias, however, hits Hector in the chest with a large stone and Hector drops in the dust. The Trojans surround their stricken hero with their shields and carry him from the field, and the fighting rages on without him.

As Zeus wakes to see the Achaians' success and Hector dazed and vomiting blood, he confronts Hera with her treachery, but she denies that she has led Poseidon against the Trojans (**book fifteen**). Zeus then sends her to Olympus to tell Iris that she must summon Poseidon away from the battle and to tell Apollo that he must heal Hector so he can rejoin the fight and that he must then "drive strengthless / panic into the Achaians." Zeus goes on with significant foretelling: Hector shall kill even Zeus' own son, Sarpedon, and Achilles' beloved companion, Patroklos, which will drive Achilles back to the battle until the Achaians finally win. But until all this happens, Zeus says, he will not let any god help the Achaians.

At Olympus the other gods greet Hera, who tells them they should heed Zeus or suffer as Ares has by the death of his son. On hearing this, Ares sets off to avenge himself against the Achaians, but Athena stops him, fearing Zeus' anger. Then Iris and Apollo move to obey Zeus' orders, although Poseidon leaves the battle only reluctantly.

The Trojans now advance in a pack, with Apollo leading the way and driving terror into the Achaians. Apollo himself helps destroy the Achaians' bastions, like a "little boy" who "makes sand towers . . . / and then, still playing, with hands and feet ruins them." As Patroklos, sitting far away, sees this, he determines to rouse Achilles back into the fight. Aias and his brother, Teucer, lead the Achaians against the Trojans, but Hector forces the Achaians back to their ships.

Patroklos, moved to tears as he watches, chides Achilles for his anger and begs to be given his armor so that, seeming to be Achilles, he might frighten the Trojans and encourage the Achaians (**book sixteen**). Achilles agrees but insists that Patroklos only force the Trojans back from the ships and go no further, "for fear some one of the everlasting gods on Olympus / might crush" him. As they speak, Aias can hold out no longer and Hector sets his ship on fire. Seeing the flames, Achilles tells Patroklos to prepare for battle, and Patroklos arrays himself in Achilles' greaves, corselet, helmet, and sword—all but the spear, which only Achilles can handle. Achilles then prepares his troops and prays to Zeus that Patroklos beat the Trojans away and return unwounded; Zeus hears him but grants only half his prayer.

The Trojans are shaken when they see what they believe to be Achilles back in the battle. Patroklos slaughters many Trojans and faces the great hero Sarpedon. At this point Zeus weeps "tears of blood" for the sake of his son but knows that he cannot be saved. The heroes meet, and Patroklos hurls his spear, striking Sarpedon "where the beating heart is closed in the arch of the muscle." Sarpedon falls and, dying, bids his comrades not to let the Achaians strip his armor. The battle then rages over his body as Zeus, watching, ponders how to bring about Patroklos' death. He decides first to let the Achaians advance, but when they finally strip away Sarpedon's armor Zeus instructs Apollo to carry off his son, wash him, and place him in the hands of Sleep and Death, who will take him to his homeland for burial.

Meanwhile Patroklos presses on, and the Achaians are on the verge of taking Troy when Apollo warns Patroklos to give way, and then tells Hector to try to kill him. Both sides fight throughout the afternoon until finally Patroklos, having charged three times upon the Trojans, on the fourth is stalked by Apollo himself, the god moving through the battle "shrouded in deep mist." In a famous scene, Apollo attacks Patroklos, striking from his head the "four-horned and hollow-eyed" helmet, which rolls beneath the horses' hoofs in a terrible prefiguring of the hero's own fall. The spear is then splintered in his hands, the shield drops from his shoulders, and "his shining body goes nerveless." A lesser warrior wounds him, and Hector easily rides in and cuts him down. So as the book ends, the first central heroes have died—and, dying, Patroklos warns Hector that he too will not live long.

The body of Patroklos is the focus of **book seventeen**. Menelaus defends the corpse from the Trojans until Apollo rouses Hector. As Hector approaches, Menelaus reluctantly withdraws to seek Aias' help. Hector strips Achilles' armor from Patroklos' body but is stopped from taking and dismembering the body itself by Menelaus and Aias. He then puts on the armor but is rebuked by Zeus for wearing "the immortal armour / of a surpassing man." Zeus says that he will grant Hector renewed strength but that Hector will "not come home out of the fighting." Hector instills his men with even greater fury and determination to take Patroklos' body.

Aias and Menelaus now rally the Achaians, but Hector leads another attack, forcing the Achaians again to withdraw from the body. Aias exhorts them to persevere, and the Achaians are gaining against the Trojans when Apollo inspires Aeneas. The bloody battle rages throughout the day, yet Achilles still does not know that his companion is dead. The Achaians, seeing that Zeus is helping the Trojans, deliberate on how they can at least wrest away Patroklos' body and carry the sad message to Achilles. Later, Athena breathes new strength into Menelaus, but at the same time Apollo goads Hector; Zeus shrouds the battlefield in mist and gives the Trojans victory. At last Menelaus sends a messenger to Achilles with the news, and then he himself, with the help of Aias and others, finally carries Patroklos' body out of the fighting and back to the ships.

The battle continues as Achilles learns of Patroklos' death (**book eighteen**). The "black cloud of sorrow" closes on him, and he lets out a cry so loud that his mother hurries from the depths of the sea to comfort him. Achilles swears that he will overtake and kill "that killer of a dear life, / Hector." At this Thetis weeps, because she knows that Achilles' death will occur shortly after Hector's. Telling her son to wait until she has brought him new armor, she departs. But Iris, sent by Hera, tells Achilles to go into battle immediately; even without armor, she says, the very sight of him will scare the Trojans and bring new life to the Achaians. He rises, and Athena "about his head [circles] / a golden cloud, and [kindles] from it a flame far-shining." The Trojans are terrified, and, as night falls, the Achaians begin to mourn the dead Patroklos. The Trojans, meanwhile, debate their strategies, with Poulydamas advising a retreat and Hector angrily denying the threat posed by Achilles.

Thetis now finds Hephaistos working at his bellows and begs him to make new armor for her son. He begins at once, and the description of the shield he forges for Achilles is among the most famous elements in the epic. Elaborately detailed, it depicts the range of the known cosmos, with "the sky, and the sea's water, / and the tireless sun, and the moon, . . . [and] two cities of mortal men," with marriages and civic life taking place in one, while the other is besieged by war; beyond the cities are scenes of agricultural life, both harmonious and violent; and around the whole rim of the shield is portrayed the "Ocean River." When Hephaistos finishes, he also forges a corselet and helmet and gives all these to Thetis.

The following dawn, Thetis finds Achilles with the Achaians, still mourning Patroklos (**book nineteen**). As she gives him the fearful armor, all the others tremble, but Achilles accepts it somberly. She then instills in him new strength and courage, and he addresses the Achaians and offers reconciliation with Agamemnon. Agamemnon in turn admits that he was wrong in dishonoring Achilles but insists that he was not responsible, blaming instead "Delusion . . . the elder daughter of Zeus, the accursed / who deludes all." He promises to deliver the gifts pledged earlier, but Achilles now brushes aside the issue in his eagerness to fight. Odysseus asks Achilles not to send the men into battle without eating, but Achilles' desire for revenge is so great that he wants to go immediately: "Food and drink mean nothing to my heart / but blood does, and slaughter. . . ." Odysseus insists, however, that things be done in their proper order. So the gifts, including Briseis, are brought out, and Agamemnon sacrifices a boar and prays to Zeus while the men stand "in silence and in order of station, and [listen] to their king," who swears that he never touched the woman. The gifts, women, and horses resume their proper places as the men return each to his own ship to eat—the whole scene suggesting the resumption of order broken by Agamemnon at the epic's outset.

At last, full of desire for battle, Achilles puts on his armor and, shining like the sun, drives his immortal horses to the front lines. Yet they, given voice by Hera, warn him that they will keep him safe for now but that soon he will be killed by a god and a mortal. To this Achilles says, "But for all that I will not stop till the Trojans have had enough of my fighting."

Zeus then summons the gods to Olympus and tells them that, as Achilles has returned to the battle, they may now help either side (**book twenty**). So they fully enter the fighting: Hera, Athena, Poseidon, Hermes, and Hephaistos with the Achaians; Ares, Apollo, Artemis, Leto, and Aphrodite with the Trojans. And such is "the crash that [sounds] as the gods [come] driving together / in wrath" that even the god of the underworld screams in fear. Meanwhile Achilles is determined to confront Hector. Seeing this, Apollo rallies Aeneas and puts new courage into his heart so he will hunt Achilles, each the son of a goddess. Meeting, they shout insults and lengthy boasts until Aeneas hurls his spear, but without success. Achilles, in turn, launches his spear, which lodges in Aeneas' shield but does no harm, although Aeneas is afraid. Achilles now rushes at him with his "tearing sword," and Aeneas seizes a huge stone—but the action is temporarily frozen as Poseidon deliberates interference. The god then pulls Achilles' spear from Aeneas' shield and drops it at Achilles' feet, hurling Aeneas from the scene at the same time. Achilles recognizes the god's intervention and, though angered by Aeneas' disappearance, is filled with new fervor. He goes among the Achaians and exhorts them to break the Trojan ranks.

Hector, however, likewise encourages the Trojans to endure, although Apollo warns him not to confront Achilles alone. He heeds the warning, and the battle continues, with Achilles destroying many men. Finally, Achilles kills one of Hector's brothers, and Hector can hold himself back no longer. The two—the greatest heroes of either side—confront each other, and although each attacks well, Athena and Apollo protect their favorites. Instead, Achilles sweeps on in a brutal rage and kills many in his path, "straining to win glory, his invincible hands spattered with bloody filth."

Achilles advances against the Trojans, pursuing many into the Xanthos River and slaughtering them there like "a huge-gaping dolphin" chasing fish (**book twenty-one**). In one of the epic's most spectacular scenes, the river Skamandros itself rises up to protest being "crammed with corpses" and then sends wave after wave to beat against Achilles and pursue him, "[cutting] the ground from under his feet." Achilles calls out to Zeus for mercy against this "dismal death," and Poseidon and Athena come to his aid. The river doubles its forces, though, and Achilles is almost lost in the waves before Hera finally cries to Hephaistos to save him with a fire that burns the corpses, the trees and clover along the river banks, the eels and fish trying to escape from the roiling water, and finally the water itself.

Meanwhile the other gods clash even more fiercely. Ares stabs at Athena, but she hits him with a huge stone so that he falls, "spread over seven acres." Aphrodite then tries to lead him away, but Hera, seeing this, sends Athena after her as well, and soon Aphrodite too lies "sprawled on the generous earth." Poseidon confronts Apollo, who declines to fight the older god, which in turn provokes Artemis, whose angry words are heard by Hera, who boxes her before the younger flees. Artemis' mother, Leto, follows her and finds her weeping at Zeus' knees.

As the chaos among the gods intensifies, Achilles' rage goes unchecked. When the other gods return exhausted to Olympus, Apollo goes to Troy, where Priam is ordering the city's gates opened so that the Trojans can escape inside. Apollo inspires one Trojan in particular, Agenor, to attack Achilles, but still the hero is unhurt. Then, clouding Achilles' vision, Apollo himself assumes the form of Agenor (whom he hides in mist) as a decoy for Achilles so the Trojans can escape into the city.

The Trojans gather inside the walls but "his deadly fate [holds] Hector shackled" so that he remains outside (**book twenty-two**). Apollo now reveals himself to the vexed Achilles, who stalks back toward the city. Upon seeing Achilles approach, Priam beseeches Hector to come to safety, already envisioning the downfall of his city, his "daughters dragged away captive," the "innocent children taken and dashed to the ground," and himself ripped raw by his own dogs. Hekabe weeps too and pleads with her son to come inside. But Hector remains outside, although he ponders ways to escape and imagines laying down his arms and promising to give up Helen, all her possessions, and even Troy's wealth. Achilles' fearsome intractability, though, and Hector's own shame make him face the confrontation to see "to which one the Olympian grants the glory."

Achilles charges, and Hector, suddenly terrified, flees. In one of the epic's most famous scenes, the gods look on as the two are caught in a deadly race around the walls of Troy, running "for the life of Hector": "As in a dream a man is not able to follow one who runs / from him, nor can the runner escape." But when they have circled the city three times, Zeus balances the scales of their lives and finds that the death of Hector is heavier. Apollo now abandons him. Ordered by Zeus, Athena tells Achilles to stop chasing and instead demand combat. Then, disguised as Hector's brother Deiphobos, she convinces Hector that the two should fight Achilles together. So Hector turns, faces Achilles, and tries to swear a mutual oath that the winner will not defile the other's corpse. Achilles will swear nothing.

Achilles hurls his spear but misses Hector, and Athena returns his spear. Hector hits Achilles' shield but does not pierce it, so he calls to Deiphobos for another spear—only to find to his horror that Deiphobos is not there. "No use," Hector then says. "[T]here is no way out." Achilles continues his attack, "eyeing Hector's splendid body, to see where it might best / give way," but the very sight of his own armor stripped from Patroklos' body and now worn by Hector enrages Achilles even more. He drives his spear through the armor's one gap, at the neck, and Hector drops in the dust. He beseeches Achilles once more to return his body for burning, but Achilles refuses. In his dying words, Hector tells him that Paris and Apollo will slay him at the city gates.

Achilles boasts over Hector's body as the Achaians gaze upon its "imposing beauty." Then, in his rage to shame the glorious figure, Achilles cuts holes between the ankles and heels, draws a thong through, and drags the corpse back to the Achaians. As Hector's head "that was once so handsome" is dragged in the dust, Priam, Hekabe, and all of Troy wail with grief. Only Andromache, at that moment drawing her husband's bath, does not yet know. But hearing the cries she guesses, rushes to the walls, and sees.

The focus shifts abruptly to Patroklos' funeral (**book twenty-three**). The Achaians try to convince Achilles, who has begun elaborate rites in honor of his friend, to wash off the gore of battle, but he refuses, intent on grieving. At last Achilles falls asleep, only to be visited by the spirit of Patroklos, who rebukes him for not burning and burying his body yet, warns him that he too will soon die, and requests that their bones remain together in death as in life. Still sleeping, Achilles tries to embrace his friend, but the spirit slips away like vapor. Achilles awakes sorrowing that in Hades "there is left something, / a soul and an image, but there is no real heart of life in it." He stirs the Achaians to mourn, and they then set about constructing a pyre on which, with lamentation and ceremony, Patroklos' body is burned. The next morning Achilles instructs the Achaians to set aside the bones of Patroklos in an urn and explains where and how they should bury the bones along with his own. Then he holds funeral games among the Achaians in Patroklos' honor, distributing splendid prizes.

The previous books having focused upon the body of Patroklos, the **last book** turns to that of Hector. After Patroklos' funeral, Achilles, unable to sleep for weeping, drags Hector's body around his friend's tomb and then throws the dead man face-down in the dust. But the gods, looking on, are filled with compassion and disturbed by this outrage. As in the epic's opening, Apollo is the instrument of balance, first protecting Hector's body from mutilation, then appealing to the others to let him be properly buried. Zeus sends Iris to tell Priam to claim his son's body and has Thetis instruct her son to relent.

Despite Hekabe's frightened appeals, Priam prepares elaborate gifts to ransom his son. She brings wine to pour a libation to Zeus before Priam leaves, and Zeus rewards them by sending a black eagle as a good omen. Priam then sets out into the darkness toward the Achaian camps. Zeus, pitying the old man, sends Hermes to guide him safely, and at last they reach Achilles' dwelling. Priam enters and kisses "the hands / that were dangerous and manslaughtering," and, reminding Achilles of his own old father, begs him to return Hector's body. In a scene of quiet humanity, Achilles is stirred to pity "for the grey head and the grey beard" and grieves with the old man for their separate losses. Achilles then has his men wash and anoint Hector's body, and himself lifts it into a litter. The two then peaceably eat, and Achilles has a bed made for Priam, agreeing to the old king's request for a cease-fire while the Trojans mourn Hector. Finally, all gods and mortals sleep—all but Hermes. He wakes Priam and takes him and his servant away undetected.

Upon their return, the Trojans greet them in sorrow and begin the funeral rituals. Mirroring Hector's earlier entry into the city, his final return is met by the three women: Andromache, Hekabe, and Helen. Andromache leads the weeping, saying,

> [F]or me passing all others is left the bitterness
> and the pain, for you did not die in bed, and stretch your arms to me,
> nor tell me some last intimate word that I could remember
> always, all the nights and days of my weeping for you.

Soon she is joined by Hekabe and the other Trojan women. Finally Helen weeps over Hector's body, declaring, "There was no other in [Troy] / who was kind to me, and my friend; all others shrank when they saw me." The *Iliad* ends as the Trojans, in the respite granted by Achilles, burn and bury their hero. ✤

—*Elizabeth Beaudin*
Yale University

(Above translations are Richmond Lattimore's.)

List of Characters

Achaians

Achilles is the focal point of the *Iliad,* which tells of his anger at being dishonored by Agamemnon, leader of the Achaian forces. The daughter of a sea goddess, Thetis, Achilles invoked divine assistance to throw the war against the Achaians in retribution. But after his beloved friend, Patroklos, has been killed by the Trojan hero Hector, Achilles returns to the fight. Throughout the epic Achilles shows his emotions and his strength equally.

Agamemnon, brother of Menelaus and leader of the Achaians, provokes the conflict in the epic by refusing to return his concubine, Chryseis, unless he can replace her with Achilles' own mistress, Briseis. Although stubborn, Agamemnon usually yields after listening to the advice of others, such as Nestor.

Menelaus, Agamemnon's brother and a chief king of the Achaians, has most at stake in the war, which was launched to retrieve his wife, Helen.

Patroklos is Achilles' beloved comrade, who returns to the battle when the Trojans push the Achaians to their ships. His killing by Hector propels Achilles to avenge him.

Aias (son of Telamon) is a distinguished warrior, outstanding for his size.

Diomedes is a distinguished warrior aided by Athena.

Nestor is a wise elder statesman and rhetorician.

Odysseus is a resourceful and perspicacious king. Unlike Agamemnon, Odysseus is certain that the Achaians will win; and although younger than Nestor, he too offers wise counsel.

Trojans

Hector, a prince of Troy and its greatest warrior, defends his people until, having killed Patroklos, he is killed by Achilles. In some ways Achilles' double, Hector is imbued with as much emotion and nobility as ferocity. The eventual ransom and burial of his body form the epic's somber end.

Paris, a prince of Troy, instigates the war with the Achaians by absconding with Menelaus' wife, Helen. Although often described by other characters as idle or licentious, Paris is occasionally valorous in battle.

Aeneas, one of the bravest warriors and destined to continue the Trojan line once the city has fallen, stands by Hector with help and encouragement.

Deiphobos is Hector's brother, impersonated by Athena to deceive Hector in his final confrontation with Achilles.

Poulydamas often tries to dissuade Hector from reckless action.

Sarpedon, Zeus' son and a mighty warrior, is killed by Patroklos.

Priam, the Trojan king, witnesses the death of his sons, the most distinguished among them Hector, whose body he ransoms.

Hekabe, the Trojan queen, is the wife of Priam and mother of Hector, Paris, and many other doomed Trojans.

Andromache weeps at the sight of her husband, Hector, when he leaves for battle and when his body is returned to her as the *Iliad* ends.

Helen, the reputed cause of the Trojan War, is hated and grudgingly admired by both sides. At the epic's end, she cries for Hector, the only Trojan to have befriended her.

Gods

Zeus, king of the Olympian gods, is fundamentally pro-Trojan but agrees to honor Achilles and sacrifice his own son, Sarpedon, and favorite, Hector.

Thetis is a goddess of the sea and Achilles' mother. Her request to Zeus that her son be honored by the gods, if not by men, incites the epic's chief action.

Hera, queen of the gods, intercedes often and ruthlessly on the Achaians' behalf, even deceiving Zeus to do so.

Apollo helps the Trojans, entering the combat physically, as when he strips Patroklos of his helmet and shield.

Athena helps the Achaians as often as possible, protecting Diomedes in particular and attacking fellow gods.

Ares, another Trojan supporter, often feels the brunt of Athena's and Hera's devotion to the Achaians.

Aphrodite sides with the Trojans, although she is skilled in love rather than in war and is wounded more than once.

Poseidon, god of the sea, supports the Achaians and only reluctantly leaves the battle at Zeus' bidding.

Hephaistos supports the Achaians and forges intricate armor for Achilles at Thetis' request.

Hermes, a guide and messenger of the gods, safely leads Priam to Achilles' tent to ransom Hector's body. ✤

Critical Views

DIONYSIUS OF HALICARNASSUS ON HOMER'S SKILL AT WORD-PAINTING

[Dionysius of Halicarnassus, a Greek historian and critic who settled in Rome around 30 B.C.E., was the author of many works, including *Roman Antiquities* and a number of critical essays. In the following extract, Dionysius praises the skill with which Homer matches his words to the emotions they are conveying.]

The most elegant writers of poetry or prose have understood these facts well, and both arrange their words by weaving them together with deliberate care, and with elaborate artistic skill adapt the syllables and the letters to the emotions which they wish to portray. Homer does this often, as, for example, when describing a sea-shore exposed to the wind's blasts, he wants to express the ceaseless roar, and does so by the drawing-out of the syllables:

> The jutting shores resound, the foaming tide is held at bay.

Or again, when the Cyclops has been blinded, to express the greatness of his anguish and his hands' slow search for the door of the cavern, he says:

> The Cyclops utters groan on groan in the throes of anguish sore
> With hands slow-groping.

And when in another place he wishes to portray a long and deeply earnest prayer:

> Nor can the archer-god Apollo's passionate prayers avail
> Though grovelling low at Father Zeus the aegis-bearer's feet.

Countless such lines are to be found in Homer, representing length of time, bodily size, extremity of emotion, immobility of position, or some similar effect, by nothing more than the artistic arrangement of the syllables; while other lines are wrought in the opposite way to portray brevity, speed, urgency, and the like. For example:

> Convulsively wailing to her handmaids she cried

and

> And scared were the charioteers beholding that tireless flame

In the first of these the halting of ⟨Andromache's⟩ breath is indicated, and her loss of control of her voice; in the second, the mental distraction ⟨of the charioteers⟩ and the unexpectedness of their terror. The effect in both cases is due to the reduction of the number of syllables and words.
—Dionysius of Halicarnassus, *On Literary Composition* (c. 20 B.C.E.), *The Critical Essays,* ed. and tr. Stephen Usher (Cambridge, MA: Harvard University Press, 1985), Vol. 2, pp. 109, 111, 113

ALEXANDER POPE ON HOMER'S IMAGINATION

[Alexander Pope (1688–1744), the leading British poet of his age, translated both the *Iliad* and the *Odyssey* into English. In the following extract from the preface to the *Iliad,* Pope praises the bountiful imagination (or "invention") of Homer, although later in the preface Pope finds Homer to be somewhat unruly in style and diction.]

Homer is universally allowed to have had the greatest invention of any writer whatever. The praise of judgment Virgil has justly contested with him, and others may have their pretensions as to particular excellencies; but his invention remains yet unrivaled. Nor is it a wonder if he has ever been acknowledged the greatest of poets, who most excelled in that which is the very foundation of poetry. It is the invention that in different degrees distinguishes all great geniuses; the utmost stretch of human study, learning, and industry, which masters everything besides, can never attain to this. It furnishes Art with all her materials, and without it judgment itself can at best but *steal wisely.* For Art is only like a prudent steward that lives on managing the riches of Nature. Whatever praises may be given to works of judgment, there is not even a single beauty in them but is owing to the invention; as in the most regular gardens, however Art may carry the greatest appearance, there is not a plant or flower but is the gift of Nature. The first can only reduce the beauties of the latter into a more obvious figure, which the common eye may better take in and is therefore more entertained with. And perhaps the reason why most critics are inclined to prefer a judicious and methodical genius to a great and fruitful one is because they find it easier for themselves to pursue their observations through an uniform and bounded walk of Art than to comprehend the vast and various extent of Nature.

Our author's work is a wild paradise, where, if we cannot see all the beauties so distinctly as in an ordered garden, it is only because the number of them is infinitely greater. 'Tis like a copious nursery which contains the seeds and first productions of every kind, out of which those who followed him have but selected some particular plants, each according to his fancy, to cultivate and beautify. If some things are too luxuriant, it is owing to the richness of the soil; and if others are not arrived to perfection or maturity, it is only because they are overrun and oppressed by those of a stronger nature.

It is to the strength of this amazing invention we are to attribute that unequaled fire and rapture which is so forcible in Homer that no man of a true poetical spirit is master of himself while he reads him. What he writes is of the most animated nature imaginable; everything moves, everything lives and is put in action. If a council be called or a battle fought, you are not coldly informed of what was said or done as from a third person; the reader is hurried out of himself by the force of the poet's imagination and turns in one place to a hearer, in another to a spectator. The course of his verses resembles that of the army he describes, Οἱ δ' ἄρ' ἴσαν ὡς εἴ τε πυρὶ χθὼν πᾶσα νέμοιτο. "They pour along like a fire that sweeps the whole earth before it." 'Tis however remarkable that his fancy, which is everywhere vigorous, is not discovered immediately at the beginning of his poem in its fullest splendor; it grows in the progress both upon himself and others, and becomes on fire like a chariot-wheel, by its own rapidity. Exact disposition, just thought, correct elocution, polished numbers may have been found in a thousand; but this poetical *fire*, this *vivida vis animi*, in a very few. Even in works where all those are imperfect or neglected, this can overpower criticism and make us admire even while we disapprove. Nay, where this appears, though attended with absurdities, it brightens all the rubbish about it, till we see nothing but its own splendor. This *fire* is discerned in Virgil, but discerned as through a glass, reflected, and more shining than warm, but everywhere equal and constant. In Lucan and Statius it bursts out in sudden, short, and interrupted flashes; in Milton it glows like a furnace kept up to an uncommon fierceness by the force of art; in Shakespeare it strikes before we are aware, like an accidental fire from Heaven; but in Homer, and in him only, it burns everywhere clearly and everywhere irresistibly.

—Alexander Pope, "Preface to the Translation of the *Iliad*" (1715), *The Literary Criticism of Alexander Pope,* ed. Bertrand A. Goldgar (Lincoln: University of Nebraska Press, 1965), pp. 107–8

John Addington Symonds on the Structural and Thematic Integrity of the *Iliad*

[John Addington Symonds (1840–1893) was a fellow of Magdalen College, Oxford, and a prominent British critic and scholar. Among his works are *The Renaissance in Italy* (1875–86) and *Christopher Marlowe* (1881). In this extract from *Studies of the Greek Poets* (1873–76), Symonds counters the assertions that the *Iliad* was written by more than one person, pointing out its structural and thematic integrity.]

It is the sign of a return to healthy criticism that scholars are beginning to acknowledge that the *Iliad* may be one poem— that is to say, no mere patchwork of ballads and minor epics put together by some diaskeuast in the age of Pisistratus, but the work of a single poet, who surveyed his creation as an artist, and was satisfied with its unity. We are not bound to pronounce an opinion as to whether this poet was named Homer, whether Homer ever existed, and, if so, at what period of the world's history he lived. We are not bound to put forward a complete view concerning the college of Homeridæ, from which the poet must have arisen, if he did not found it. Nor, again, need we deny that the *Iliad* itself presents unmistakable signs of having been constructed in a great measure out of material already existing in songs and romances dear to the Greek nation in their youth, and familiar to the poet. The aesthetic critic finds no difficulty in conceding, nay, is eager to claim, a long genealogy through antecedent, now forgotten, poems for the *Iliad*. But about this, of one thing, at any rate, he will be sure, after due experience of the tests applied by Wolf and his followers, that a great artist gave its present form to the *Iliad,* that he chose from the whole Trojan tale a central subject for development, and that all the episodes and collateral matter with which he enriches his epic were arranged by him with a view to the effect that he had calculated.

What, then, was this central subject, which gives the unity of a true work of art to the *Iliad?* We answer, the person and the character of Achilles. It is not fanciful to say, with the old grammarians of Alexandria, that the first line of the poem sets forth the whole of its action—

Sing, goddess, the wrath of Achilles, son of Peleus.

The wrath of Achilles, and the consequences of that wrath in the misery of the Greeks, left alone to fight without their fated hero; the death of Patroclus, caused by his sullen anger; the energy of Achilles, reawakened by his remorse for his friend's death; and the consequent slaughter of Hector, form the whole of the simple structure of the *Iliad*. This seems clear enough when we analyze the conduct of the poem.

The first book describes the quarrel of Achilles with Agamemnon and his secession from the war. The next seven books and a half, from the second to the middle of the ninth, are occupied with the fortunes of the Greeks and Trojans in the field, the exploits of Diomede and Ajax, and Hector's attack upon the camp. In the middle of the ninth book Achilles reappears upon the scene. Agamemnon sends Ulysses and Phoenix to entreat him to relax his wrath and save the Greeks; but the hero remains obdurate. He has resolved that his countrymen shall pay the uttermost penalty for the offense of their king. The poet having foredetermined that Achilles shall only consent to fight in order to revenge Patroclus, is obliged to show the inefficacy of the strongest motives from without; and this he has effected by the episode of the embassy. The tenth book relates the night attack upon the camp of the Trojan allies and the theft of the horses of Rhesus. The next five books contain a further account of the warfare carried on among the ships between the Achaians and their foes. It is in the course of these events that Patroclus comes into prominence. We find him attending on the wounded Eurypylus and warning Achilles of the imminent peril of the fleet. At last, in the sixteenth book, when Hector has carried fire to the ship of Protesilaus, Achilles commands Patroclus to assume the armor of Peleus and lead his Myrmidons to war. The same book describes the repulse of Hector and the death of Patroclus, while the seventeenth is taken up with the fight for the body of Achilles' friend. But from the eighteenth onward the true hero assumes his rank as protagonist, making us feel that what has gone before has only been a preface to his action. His seclusion from the war has not only enabled the poet to vary the interest by displaying other characters, but has also proved the final intervention of Achilles to be absolutely necessary for the success of the Greek army. All the threads of interest are gathered together and converge on him. Whatever we have learned concerning the situation of the war, the characters of the chiefs, and the jealousies of the gods, now serves to dignify his single person and to augment the terror he inspires. With his mere shout he dislodges the Trojans from the camp. The divine arms of Hephæstus are fashioned for him, and forth he goes to drive the foe like mice before him. Then he contends with Simoeis and Scamander, the river-gods. Lastly, he slays Hector. What follows in the twenty-third and twenty-fourth books seems to be intended as a repose from the vehement action and high-wrought passion of the preceeding five. Patroclus is buried, and his funeral games are celebrated. Then, at the very end, Achilles appears before us in the interview with Priam, no longer as a petulant spoiled child or fiery barbarian chief, but as a hero, capable of sacrificing his still fierce passion for revenge to the nobler emotion of reverence for the age and sorrow of the sonless king.

The centralization of interest in the character of Achilles constitutes the grandeur of the *Iliad*. It is also by this that the *Iliad* is distinguished from all the narrative epics of the world.
—John Addington Symonds, *Studies of the Greek Poets* (1873–76; rpt. New York: Harper & Brothers, 1880), pp. 91–94

JOHN A. SCOTT ON THE WRATH OF ACHILLES

[John A. Scott (1867–1947) was an American student of religion and classical antiquity who wrote *The Unity of Homer* (1921), *Socrates and Christ* (1928), and *Homer and His Influence* (1925), from which this extract is taken. Here, Scott examines the central theme of the *Iliad,* the wrath of Achilles, and illustrates the rich material Homer left to the Western literary canon.]

The first word of the *Iliad* is "Wrath" which reveals at once the kernel of the poem, since the *Iliad* does not depend on the fate of Achilles, but solely on his wrath. There are no unanswered questions concerning this wrath, its origin, its course, or its results; but the death of Achilles, the return of Helen, the end of the war seem hardly nearer than when the poem began. The historical element in the *Iliad* is thus but slight, even if it does concern an actual war.

The speeches of the quarrel scene and of the embassy, the pleadings of Thetis with Zeus, the parting of Hector from Andromache, the making of the shield, the games, the father begging for the delivery of the corpse of his son are all poetic creations, unhampered by time or place.

Recent excavations made at Troy and geographical surveys in the Troad are of great value and prove that the poet chose a real city and an actual landscape for his setting, also that he was describing a civilization that had once existed, but, even granting all this, Homer has none the less given to "airy nothing a local habitation and a name."

A real Mt. Ida there must have been, but the scene thereon between Zeus and Hera is still mythical; genuine is the wall of Troy, but Helen's appearance at its summit and Hector's parting from Andromache are merely the creation of the poet's fancy.

Into the story of Achilles' anger the poet has woven most of the great human emotions and has endowed all his actors with an individuality that has never been surpassed. It is easier to enter into familiar companionship with the great Homeric creations than with Miltiades, Themistocles, Thucydides, or with most of the historical characters of Greece. We know Nestor better than we know even so famous a man as Pericles, in spite of Thucydides, Plutarch, and the comic poets.

The *Iliad* introduced to literature such outstanding figures as Agamemnon, Achilles, Hector, Paris, Priam, Diomede, Nestor, Odysseus, Helen, Hecuba, and Andromache. Each appears as a distinct personality and has ever since preserved the Homeric features.
—John A. Scott, *Homer and His Influence* (Boston: Marshall, Jones & Co., 1925), pp. 41–42

C. M. Bowra on the Heroic in Homer

[C. M. Bowra (1898–1971) was a fellow of Wadham College, Oxford, and a prolific critic of ancient and modern literature. Among his books are *The Greek Experience* (1957), *Periclean Athens* (1971), and *Tradition and Design in the* Iliad (1930), from which the following extract is taken. Here, Bowra explores Homer's idea of heroism in the *Iliad* and relates it to heroic themes in other Western literary traditions.]

A man's ⟨. . .⟩ life is in battle, and for the risks of battle his whole life must be prepared. Hence all Homer's heroes are brave. Even Paris, idler though he is, is stung into courage by Hector's words. The gods may cry from pain, but men take their wounds without flinching. But courage is not enough. Battle demands that men must stand together, and the central tenet of Homeric morality is based on this need. In his notion of αιδως Homer gives the clue. αιδως, as Professor ⟨Gilbert⟩ Murray has said, 'is what you feel about an act of your own', but it only has a meaning in relation to what you do to others. It is respect for your fellow men. It applies first and foremost to the men you commonly meet, to superiors and inferiors, to strangers and beggars, to the gods and to the old. The martial qualities needed some admixture of tenderness and decency to preserve them, and this was found in the notion of αιδως. Because of it men refrain from excessive cruelty, and help each other in their needs. This quality which Homer gives to his heroes is particularly noticeable in the *Iliad* itself. He does not spare us horrors—they are part of his tragic scheme—but he is careful never to condone acts of injustice or of cruelty. The *Iliad* is profoundly moral, just because Homer has absorbed the morality of the heroic age. To claim that this singleness of moral outlook is the work of continual expurgation is to misunderstand the temper of an age of heroes. Such an age has its own high standards based on a man's sense of his own dignity. They differ, as might be expected, from other systems of morality, but they are not less exalted. Homer's ethics, though taught by Athenian educators, are not the ethics of Periclean Athens. For him the standard is the individual, but for Pericles it is the city. Of national or racial boundaries he takes little heed. It does not matter that Hector is a barbarian, provided he behaves as a true soldier. Nor has Homer the Athenian view of women, based on their position in an all-absorbing state. His individualism is perfectly logical, and he treats Helen and Andromache with the seriousness and understanding which he gives to Achilles. They have their part in life, and that is enough for him, just as the Icelandic poets were content to portray with complete candour and dignity their tragic heroines, Gudrun and Brynhild. The heroic age honoured its women and gave them power. So Homer was saved from making them too womanly, as Euripides sometimes did, or from raising them to that sublime selflessness to which Sophocles raised Antigone. Still less has Homer any sympathy with those waves of self-denial and puritanism which occasionally swept over later Greece. Such eccentricities are alien to the spirit of an heroic age. The Trojan War was fought for a woman's sake, and over a woman Achilles quarrelled with Agamemnon. The facts of sex are frankly stated, and there is no glorification of purity or self-abnegation. The sword that lay between Tristram and Iseult is unheard of in Homer. But love plays a small part in the story, and though this may be due partly to the exigencies of camp life, it is due much more to heroic standards of conduct. In the *Song of Roland* there is hardly a mention of *la belle Aude,* though she is Oliver's sister and Roland's betrothed, and Beowulf's wife rests on a conjecture made in a single line. Before love became a romantic ideal for which men were ready to undergo any privation and undertake any adventure, it was held below the true dignity of a fighting man. The French romances combined the amatory ideals of Provence with the martial ideals of Normandy by creating the conception of chivalry, which made the beautiful woman the judge of honour and prowess. But in true heroic poetry this combination does not exist, and love is kept out. This is not easy in the story of a war fought about a woman, but Homer's skill is nowhere more apparent than where in a few lines he shows how men can fight about Helen. In the scene on the wall there is no trace of erotic sentimentality such as we might find in the French romances. There is the single wonderful touch of the old men finding it no matter for indignation that men should fight about her (3.156–7).

The dignity which excluded any detailed treatment of love excluded other less interesting themes. Some critics complain that Homer is lacking in those scenes of brutality and bestiality such as we might hope to find in a primitive epic. They are to be found in Hesiod, why not Homer? We might answer, for the same reason that they are found in the Old Testament but not in the old Germanic or French epics. The audience which likes horrors for their own sake is out of touch with the ideals of martial heroism. Soldiers normally see enough of horrors in their work not to want to hear more about them. But the explanation lies deeper than that. The love of horrors and obscenities lies outside the code of manners common in a heroic age. The great emphasis on personal dignity forbids any lowering of human stature by such concessions to human weakness. This does not mean that poets who write of heroic themes must entirely eschew anything horrible or disgusting. The wide scope of their stories makes such themes sooner or later inevitable. But when they come, they are either treated hastily or made the subject of tragic emotions. The saga no doubt had its crudities, and they were essential to the story, but decency forbade that the audience should be titillated by a detailed exposition of them. When Phoenix tells how he obeyed his mother and slept with his father's concubine, he says simply τῇ πιθόμην καὶ ἔρεξα (9.453) and leaves it at that. Only an age sure of its standards could achieve such a simplicity with no attempt at palliation or lubricious detail. In the heat of battle it is natural that soldiers should want to strip the dead and even to mutilate corpses. The first of these, however, was not well thought of. Achilles thought it wrong to strip Eetion (5.417), and when stripping takes place, the poet hurries over it (13.439). Mutilation of the dead was a worse offence. We have seen that his desire to maltreat Hector's body was part of the moral degradation of Achilles, and how the poet saves him from putting his threats into effect. But in one place in the saga it seems to have been too difficult for the poet to subdue the horror. When Hector dies, the Achaeans plunge their spears into his body (20.370ff.). The scene is full of tragic power and pity. The poet makes no attempt to justify the wanton exultation over the dead. He just describes the scene briefly and passes on to the worse things in store. On the other hand, when such themes were absolutely essential to the main plot, Homer is not ashamed of mentioning them, but he treats them in a moral and even tragic way. In particular this comes out in the account of Achilles, whose every lapse from heroic virtue is a new chapter in his tragedy, and whose failures, though perfectly understood, are never condoned. Apart from him hardly any hero fails in the heroic standards of behaviour. It is true that in the battle scenes there are many incidents which shock the sensitive conscience. But the heroic age felt no disgust at them. To kill your man quickly and well was a warrior's business, and there is no reason to think that Homer did not share the heroic view. Like the great poet that he was, he lamented the loss of life and youth, but he hardly seems to have felt it wrong to kill or be killed in battle. Even the killing of Dolon after he has asked for mercy does not receive his condemnation. Dolon was a spy, and there is no reason to believe that the Homeric age was kinder to spies than the twentieth century. Such an execution might be unpleasant, but Dolon was not entitled to the respect due to an enemy who fought in open battle. His action excluded him from the society of honourable men, and he was killed at once for it. In the same way the traitor Ganelon is torn to pieces by horses for his treachery, and that is the end of him. The heroic code was severe to those who did not accept its standards, and they could expect no mercy.

This code of behaviour seems to have been accepted by Homer without limitations, and it is the common code of all heroic ages. It lauds the virtues of loyalty, generosity, and courage, and it deplores meanness, cowardice, and treachery. In its own way it knows mercy, and Homer's characters are more merciful than those of the Athenian tragedians. Or rather he shrinks from themes which they treated, such as the suicide of Aias or the death of Pentheus. His standards are not theirs, because his audience was stricter in its taste and delicacy than the Athenian democracy, and he shared the taste of his time. This moral responsibility, so often absent from the Old Testament and even at times from Shakespeare, is an aristocratic virtue, derived from a high sense of dignity and decency. It had to cater for men used to privilege and responsibility, not for a Semitic populace trained to suffering, nor for the jaded or primitive tastes of the groundlings whom Shakespeare despised and placated. Hesiod's poor farmers may have liked crude tales, but Homer's audience was bred to better things and had no use for them. If the *Iliad* had really been expurgated, as is claimed, we should not have this surprising consistency of moral outlook. We might have in some ways more noble actions, but the morality of the heroic age would have suffered in the process, and it is precisely this which Homer gives us. He himself may well have rejected earlier versions of his story, which revolted his conscience or were unsuited to the ethical taste of his age. It is more than likely that in the old saga Achilles really mutilated Hector's body. But the credit for

the far nobler story in the *Iliad* must be given not to some anonymous expurgator, but to the creative genius and moral sensibility of Homer.
 —C. M. Bowra, *Tradition and Design in the* Iliad (Oxford: Clarendon Press, 1930), pp. 240–44

RACHEL BESPALOFF ON HELEN

[Rachel Bespaloff is a French literary critic and the author of *On the* Iliad (1947), from which the following extract is taken. Here, Bespaloff explores the majestic nature of Helen of Troy.]

Of all the figures in the poem she is the severest, the most austere. Shrouded in her long white veils, Helen walks across the *Iliad* like a penitent; misfortune and beauty are consummate in her and lend majesty to her step. For this royal recluse freedom does not exist; the very slave who numbers the days of oppression on some calendar of hope is freer than she. What has Helen to hope for? Nothing short of the death of the Immortals would restore her freedom, since it is the gods, not her fellow men, who have dared to put her in bondage. Her fate does not depend on the outcome of the war; Paris or Menelaus may get her, but for her nothing can really change. She is the prisoner of the passions her beauty excited, and her passivity is, so to speak, their underside. Aphrodite rules her despotically; the goddess commands and Helen bows, whatever her private repugnance. Pleasure is extorted from her; this merely makes her humiliation the more cruel. Her only resource is to turn against herself a wrath too weak to spite the gods. She seems to live in horror of herself. "Why did I not die before?" is the lament that keeps rising to her lips. Homer is as implacable toward Helen as Tolstoy is toward Anna. Both women have run away from home thinking that they could abolish the past and capture the future in some unchanging essence of love. They awake in exile and feel nothing but a dull disgust for the shrivelled ecstasy that has outlived their hope.

The promise of freedom has been sloughed off in servitude; love does not obey the rules of love but yields to some more ancient and ruder law. Beauty and death have become neighbors and from their alliance springs a necessity akin to that of force. When Helen and Anna come to and face their deteriorated dream, they can blame only themselves for having been the dupes of harsh Aphrodite. Everything they squandered comes back on them; everything they touch turns to dust or stone. In driving his heroine to suicide, Tolstoy goes beyond Christianity and rejoins Homer and the tragic poets. To them the hero's flaw is indistinguishable from the misery that arises from it. The sufferer bears it; he pays for it, but he cannot redeem it any more than he can live his life over. Clytemnestra, Orestes and Oedipus are their crimes; they have no existence outside them. Later on, the philosophers, heirs of Odysseus, introduce the Trojan horse of dialectic into the realm of tragedy. Error takes the place of the tragic fault, and the responsibility for it rests with the individual alone. With Homer, punishment and expiation have the opposite effect; far from fixing responsibility, they dissolve it in the vast sea of human suffering and the diffuse guilt of the life-process itself. A flaw in a defective universe is not quite the same thing as a sin; remorse and grace have not yet made their appearance. But it is nonetheless true that this Greek idea of a diffuse guilt represents for Homer and the tragic poets the equivalent of the Christian idea of original sin. Fed on the same reality, charged with the same weight of experience, it contains the same appraisal of existence. It too acknowledges a fall, but a fall that has no date and has been preceded by no state of innocence and will be followed by no redemption; the fall, here, is a continuous one as the life-process itself which heads forever downward into death and the absurd. In proclaiming the innocence of Becoming, Nietzsche is as far from the ancients as he is from Christianity. Where Nietzsche wants to justify, Homer simply contemplates, and the only sound that he lets ring through his lines is the plaint of the hero. If the final responsibility for the tragic guilt rests on the mischievous gods, this does not mean that guilt is nonexistent. On the contrary, there is not a page in the *Iliad* that does not emphasize its irreducible character. So fully does Helen assume it that she does not even permit herself the comfort of self-defense. In Helen, purity and

guilt mingle confusedly as they do in the vast heart of the warrior herd spread out on the plain at her feet.
—Rachel Bespaloff, *On the* Iliad (New York: Pantheon, 1947), pp. 61–64

H. T. WADE-GERY ON THE HISTORICAL BASIS OF THE *ILIAD*

[H. T. Wade-Gery was Wykeham Professor of Ancient History at Oxford University and a prominent classical scholar. He is the author of *Essays in Greek History* (1958) and coauthor of *The Athenian Tribute Lists* (1939). In this extract from *The Poet of the* Iliad (1952), Wade-Gery studies the historical basis of the *Iliad,* arguing that the poem is primarily a work of fiction.]

The Troy he knew will have been Troy VIII, or (perhaps more likely) the latest stage of VII B: a Troy known to Greeks but not yet a Greek Troy. The city which Agamemnon burnt was probably Troy VII A: between Agamemnon and Homer come four centuries of Troy VII B, a village rather than a city. These are the centuries (c. 1200–800) of the Greek collapse and slow recovery. On her relatively small scale, Greece went through what our generation has feared to see in Europe and has probably averted: a catastrophic drop in population due not to war casualties but to unchecked disease or starvation: and the total loss of civilized techniques: not only such fine techniques as the cutting of seals and gems, but basic techniques like building in permanent materials, and writing. Greece lost for a while all touch with the civilized east and even with Asia Minor: it is quite likely that no Greek went to Troy during these centuries, until shortly before Homer's time.

It was, no doubt, Aeolic Greeks from Lesbos and perhaps Kyme who first rediscovered Troy, perhaps in Homer's lifetime, perhaps a little before. They saw the ruins of Troy: they may have heard, it may be from the Trojans, that a Mycenean king had burnt it. They probably did not at first think of themselves as Agamemnon's heirs. They claimed later that their leaders had come from Mycenae, but I suspect this claim was not heard until Homer had written the *Iliad*: there is little doubt that in fact these leaders came from Boeotia or Thessaly. But like the Ionians they had in their traditional poetry memories of Mycenae and of the power which once she had deployed. I do not suppose these poems said much about Troy, but they will have said a good deal about Mycenean armies.

Such poems, and what the Trojans could tell them, and the sight of Troy itself—such, as I suppose, are the components of the legend of Troy. How much in this legend was authentic? what names survived in the traditions of either party, Greeks or Trojans? Troy was, really, burnt. This happened not far from 1200 B.C., and the Greeks appear to have been aware of this date and yet unable, out of their own memory, to bridge the gap between it and themselves. Perhaps it was the Trojans of c. 800 B.C. whose memories sufficed to measure this interval.

I do not know what language those Trojans spoke: possibly some form of Greek? In the *Hymn to Aphrodite* the Goddess visits Anchises disguised as a Phrygian princess; she tells him she can speak both languages, her own and his—Phrygian and whatever the Trojans spoke. The Trojans, then, spoke something quite distinct from Phrygian. The Phrygian element in Troy VII B, which has been inferred from one type of pottery found there, was perhaps never dominant for long, and for some time after the burning of VII A it was not there at all. Apart from this foreign element, the culture of Troy VII B derives from VII A and this again from Troy VI. Was Troy VI Greek-speaking? It seems to me not unlikely: and if so, the Greeks who rediscovered Troy about 800 B.C. may have found the language still intelligible. This would make it easier for the Trojans to contribute to the legend: but whatever they spoke, their share in creating that legend must have been considerable.

These are, I suggest, the raw materials from which the *Iliad* grew. What Greek oral poetry knew about Mycenean power: what the Trojans remembered about the burning in c. 1200 B.C.: and the Troad itself, with the remains of Priam's town.

If I may use Tolstoi's arbitrary distinction between artist and historian ('the historian has to deal with the results of an event, the artist with the fact of the event') then Homer was not a historian but an artist. He has no concern with the results of the Trojan War: he does not treat it as the title of the Greeks to Asia, he did not think of it as having in any way created the world he lived in. The Dark Ages lay between him and the event. He was not like the Highland Reaper: if *her* plaintive numbers flowed

> From old unhappy far-off things
> And battles long ago,

it was because she was descended from those who fought in them, and they and she had lived in unbroken succession in the same glen. But Homer was a colonist, and the colony was settled only recently. In *Richard II,* and in *Richard III,* Shakespeare is something of an historian: these plays deal with the start and finish of a war which had directly created the world in which the poet lived. The *Iliad* does not: rather (as I have suggested) it resembles *Macbeth.* In *Macbeth* Shakespeare has no concern with the results of the event—no serious concern: James's descent from Banquo is not a serious issue—his central concern is with the fact of the event, with the tragic experience of his characters. This means, I think, that the *Iliad* is essentially fiction: as much so (at least) as Aeschylus' *Agamemnon.* And this will be so, whether we think the tale of Troy's siege is substantially authentic or no.

As I see it, the tale is *not* substantially authentic. Hektor and Patroklos are, I believe, inventions of the poet. I do not suppose the Myrmidons mutinied at Troy. That this tale of Mycenean warfare is located at Troy (rather than Cyprus or Sicily) is due, as I think, to the accident that the great poet lived in or near north-west Asia minor. We probably all know that 'sore temptation' (which Leaf acknowledges), the temptation to believe, as we read Homer, that we read of 'a thing that really happened'. At the end of the *Coq d'Or* the Magician comes before the curtain and says to the audience, 'Very sad, isn't it? but never mind: they were none of them real.' I can bear that shock to my illusion with fortitude, but I would intensely resent it at the close of a performance of *Hamlet* or of the *Iliad.* We must guard, then, against the Skylla of wishful thinking: we must also guard against Charybdis, against the destructive virtue which insists that what we are tempted to believe is always (and therefore) wrong. Guarding against both monsters, I feel great uncertainty: Troy may have figured in Peloponnesian or Thessalian Epics, the Tale of Troy may have dominated heroic poetry for centuries before Homer. But on the whole I doubt it. I think, that is to say, that we may see here a part of Homer's creativeness (what Pope called his invention): and that his poem was a very early stage in the creation of the Tale of Troy.

But what matters more, in him as in Shakespeare, is not whether he invented his story, but that by creating his characters he creates the story afresh.
—H. T. Wade-Gery, *The Poet of the* Iliad (Cambridge: Cambridge University Press, 1952), pp. 34–37

CEDRIC H. WHITMAN ON THE STRUCTURE OF THE *ILIAD*

[Cedric H. Whitman (1916–1979) was Eliot Professor of Greek at Harvard University. He wrote *Sophocles: A Study of Heroic Humanism* (1951), *Euripides and the Full Circle of Myth* (1974), *The Heroic Paradox* (1982), and other works. In this extract from his celebrated study, *Homer and the Heroic Tradition* (1958), Whitman outlines what he believes to be the "geometric" structure of the *Iliad*.]

Not only in the associations of images and conceptions of both divine and human agents does the *Iliad* reveal its unity, but also in the matter of external form. It is now time to look at the whole poem as a series of scenes, and observe how these scenes are related to each other. As indicated before, Homeric scenes are analogous to the formulae in that they follow a typology designed to assist the singer; scenes of battle, arming, debate, supplication, lamentation, and jubilant victory bear a formal as well as an ideational resemblance to each other, though in Homer a vast degree of variety and shading has been achieved through the expansion, compression, or modification of the basic motifs. This typology of the scenes in the poetry of Homer and other oral singers has been the subject of excellent studies, and one does well to keep in mind the warning of ⟨Milman⟩ Parry not to find "falsely subtle meanings in the repetitions, as meant to recall an earlier scene where the same words were used." And yet, though such echoes would be present in all singers' efforts, one of the traits of Homer's excellence seems to have been the gift to control these echoes more than other oral poets have done. For the fixed elements of the oral style are fixed only in themselves, and out of context. In context they inevitably change color and tone, and it is by no means implausible, on the face of it, that a skilled singer, the scion of many generations of the tradition, should become aware of the subtleties of shifting context and make some effort to use them. Clearly, not every one could be controlled; moreover, it must be assumed that, like so many processes of poetic composition, much of this effort must have failed to reach the level of full consciousness. Yet, insofar as the use of balancing, or echoing, motifs contributes to the broad structure of the poems, conscious intent is probably to be assumed, since the design which emerges bears the unmistakable stamp of the waking intellect. In treating imagery, one had to deal with association and intuition; here, in the matter of structure, one is confronted by a schematized pattern, rationally worked out and altogether consistent with the observable artistic practices of the Geometric Age.

Recently, critics have begun to take account of the artistic role in Homer of the repetitive elements native to oral technique. Stereotyped themes and scenes, mere serviceable tools originally, and never more than that in the hands of a poor singer, become in Homer through varying context the vehicles of characterization and formal design. Thematic motifs, such as descriptions of sacrifices, ship-launchings, feasts, funerals, arming, and combat, are on the whole fixities of the poems, as indeed they were of the world from which the poems arose, and the recitation of such passages is as ritualistic, in a way, as were the performances of the acts which they describe. It is natural and true for a society dominated by the rigidities of ritual to represent its characteristic function in unchanging formu-

lae, normative and in a way eternal. Yet every such thematic motif may be narrated in varying degrees of fullness. It is not always easy to say what determines how far a given one may be developed, though the pace of the scene, and its purport as a whole would, of course, be governing factors. When Achilles, for instance, pours a libation and prays to Zeus for the safe return of Patroclus, the process of libation is described in minute detail, even to the cleansing of the goblet with sulfur. But this is an extremely solemn and critical moment in the plot, and it would be absurd to elaborate all the libations in the epic to the same degree. Again, the scene of the sacrifice performed at Chrysa by Odysseus on behalf of the Achaeans is one of the most complete of all descriptions of such a ceremony. Here perhaps more than mere liturgical solemnity is involved; for the arrival, debarkation, and return of the ship in which Chryseis is sent back are also lengthily described, in contrast to the more usual brief versions of such processes. The whole episode at Chrysa, in fact, has a leisurely air, in contrast to the packed dramatic scene which has preceded. And the reason probably lies in the fact that the poet here has to account for the passage of twelve days, until Zeus returns to Olympus and Thetis can present her plea for Achilles. Gaps of time are rare in epic and regularly avoided. It requires, therefore, a tour de force on Homer's part to fill an empty space when nothing particular happened. Odysseus spent only one day and one night at Chrysa, and the journey there and back probably did not take more than two more days; but the slow detailed pace of this rather neutral episode falsifies the time sense effectively, and one is prepared to accept without shock thereafter the brief summary of Achilles' inaction, and the resumptive line, "but when the twelfth dawn came," and return to the main action.
    —Cedric H. Whitman, *Homer and the Heroic Tradition* (Cambridge, MA: Harvard University Press, 1958), pp. 249–51

Denys L. Page on the Origins of the *Iliad*

[Denys L. Page is an important classical scholar who has written several controversial books, including *The Homeric Odyssey* (1955) and *Folktales in Homer's Odyssey* (1973). In this extract from *History and the Homeric Iliad* (1959), Page attempts to date the *Iliad* and to trace its roots in the oral tradition of the Greeks.]

The searcher for historical fact in the Homeric *Iliad* must begin by finding the answer to two questions. First, how far back does the Greek Epic tradition extend? It is obvious that the *Iliad* presupposes poetry of the same type over a long period of time: but *how* long? Does the tradition go back beyond the Dark Ages into the period when the glory of Mycenae was still great? Secondly, if the answer to that question is affirmative in general, how far back does this particular theme of poetry go, the story of the Achaean siege of Troy? Was it already sung by poets in the royal or noble courts of Greece in the 12th century B.C.?

The answer to the first of these questions may be stated with the utmost brevity. It has long been known that the pedigree of Greek Epic poetry ascends into the Mycenaean era. The proofs of this have been stated so often before that I do no more than repeat them summarily.

The one proof is provided by comparison of certain passages in the *Iliad* with objects discovered by excavation. *The* Iliad *and* Odyssey *describe in accurate detail places and objects which never existed in the world after the Mycenaean era.* The boar's-tusk helmet in the Tenth Book of the *Iliad* is one of the best examples: here is a distinctive and complex object, accurately described in the *Iliad* at the latest stage of its development, known to have been fashionable so far back as the 16th and 15th centuries B.C., obsolete in the 13th and extinct in the 12th century. In the words of Martin Nilsson, "such an object, the containing parts of which were of perishable materials, . . . would not have survived the centuries separating the Mycenaean Age from the beginning of the historical period. There is no explanation left but the one that the description was preserved through the lapse of time by the epic tradition."

There are several other such examples: each singly and all together they testify, beyond the possibility of confutation, that the memory of certain material objects survived from the Mycenaean era into the *Iliad,* hundreds of years after the objects themselves had disappeared from the world. This is one of the most certain and most important discoveries ever made in the field of Homeric scholarship.

The second proof is provided by the Homeric dialect. The language of the Epic is predominantly *Ionic:* but deeply embedded within it are forms and features alien to Ionic but familiar to the *Arcadian* and *Aeolic* dialects. Many but not all of these non-Ionic features are irreplaceable: that is to say, the corresponding Ionic forms are excluded by the metre.

Now the Arcadian and Aeolic dialects, as we know them, are descendants of the dialects predominant in southern and northern Hellas (respectively) in the Mycenaean period: and their presence in the Ionian Epic has generally been regarded as good evidence that the Epic must have a continuous history from the Mycenaean period onwards, when those dialects were predominant. Until recently it seemed reasonable to infer the following series of events: the Epic was originally created in Hellas by peoples who spoke the Arcadian and Aeolic dialects; when these peoples migrated to Asia Minor under pressure from the Dorians, they came into contact with other emigrants, speakers of the Ionic dialect, in Asia Minor; and these Ionians adopted the Aeolic-Arcadian Epic, made it their own, gradually transformed it both in language and in spirit into an Ionian poetry, but retained within it numerous indispensable forms and phrases, essential constituents of the verse, irreplaceable by Ionic counterparts. This account of the phenomena has recently been challenged, and the new outlook has at least in one aspect an advantage over the old.

The new theory maintains, in briefest summary, the following position: The dialect which we call *Ionic* is fundamentally akin to *Arcadian;* the peculiar features which differentiate it from other dialects as *Ionic* are all (or most) of relatively late development. In the Mycenaean period *one* dialect was predominant in southern Greece: when the Dorians occupied the Peloponnese, part of the Mycenaean population stayed at

home, part emigrated; the stay-at-homes, to be called "Arcadians," retained their dialect with comparatively little change through the Dark Ages, while the emigrants, to be called "Ionians," developed a number of new characteristics in their new homes. This theory has yet to stand the test of time; if it should prove to be true, we shall have to change our opinion about the origin of the apparent mixture of dialects in the Epic. There will be this advantage, that it will no longer be necessary to postulate a transference of the Epic from a people of one dialect to a people of another dialect. Arcadian features in the Epic will be heirlooms from the past of the Ionian people themselves; and we shall now suppose simply that the Mycenaean emigrants from the Peloponnese took their own poetry with them to Asia Minor, where it developed in the course of time, without change of owner, into the Ionian Epic.
—Denys L. Page, *History and the Homeric* Iliad (Berkeley: University of California Press, 1959), pp. 218–20

ANDRÉ MICHALOPOULOS ON HEROIC ELEMENTS IN THE *ILIAD*

[André Michalopoulos (b. 1897), formerly a professor of classical literatures and civilizations at Fairleigh Dickinson University, is the author of *Greece's Role as a Balkan and Mediterranean Power* (1942) and *Homer* (1966), from which the following extract is taken. Here, Michalopoulos examines the heroic elements of the *Iliad* and Achilles' central role.]

The Achaean hero's *amour-propre* was ingrained in him; an integral part of his personality, it had its roots in the precarious nature of the life he led. He was a king or prince with absolute authority over his followers. That authority has to be maintained by constant acts of prowess upon which the life of the tribe depended, for Aegean society was in a state of flux, and the warriors of which it was composed looked to their leaders for the advantages of profitable campaigns. It is not by chance that the sacking of a city was depicted on the shield of Achilles.

It was imperative that the chieftain at all times retain the respect of his men and uphold the honor of the tribe. To a man in Achilles' position, the public insult inflicted on him by Agamemnon was intolerable. His first reaction was to draw his sword and fight Agamemnon; he was perfectly justified by his code in doing so, and he knew that he would probably have killed the king. But at the behest of Athene, he desisted. It would have been disastrous for the Achaeans so far away from home if the commander-in-chief had been killed by his greatest ally. Achilles, therefore, retired from battle and took his fierce Myrmidons with him. To say, as many commentators do, that he "sulked" is to use an entirely unjustifiable pejorative term. What he did was the least he could and still retain his self-respect and the respect of his men because of Agamemnon's behavior. Achilles never intended to abandon the Achaeans altogether; he was a warrior too much committed to war to fulfill his threat, made in anger in Book I and repeated in a milder form in Book IX, that he might go back to his home in Phthia.

It is important to remember that Achilles was the son of a goddess. In Homer he never boasts of his semi-divine origin nor takes advantage of it. He could be proud of this origin. Nonetheless, the immense and justified pride he expresses without false modesty is in his prowess, his professional efficiency, his paramount virtues as a hero and leader of men. Excellence was nothing to be ashamed of; if it was proven and real, it was to be proclaimed—and above all it should command deferential acknowledgment. "One omen is best of all," says Homer, "ever to excell and to be superior to others." This was the heroic ideal, and upon excellence rested the hero's claim to ascendency over his subordinates and authority among his equals. In a later age we find the same respect for excellence proclaimed as an ideal of Athenian democracy. In 429 B.C. Pericles, speaking about the greatness of Athens to his people, said: "While the law secures equal justice to all alike in their private disputes, *the claim of excellence* is recognized; and when a citizen is in any way distinguished, he is preferred to the public service, not as a matter of privilege but as the reward of merit." (*Thucydides* II, 37. Tr. Benjamin Jowett, Italics mine.) Achilles was, without doubt, the most capable and the most valiant of all the Achaean warriors; he was also the most dreaded by the enemy. He was not the sort of man over whom the commander-in-chief could inconsiderately "pull rank" and take away his legitimate prize. Under the circumstances Achilles' furious reaction was quite normal.

If honor was due to Achilles because of his exceptional status as the most valuable of Agamemnon's allies and men-at-arms, it was doubly cherished by the son of Peleus because it was the only satisfaction in life left to him. In estimating the character of Achilles, it is essential to bear in mind that he was doomed to die, "slain by a god and by a man," before the capture of Troy. That his death was imminent and inescapable, he well knew. He had engaged in the war with full prophetic knowledge that he would not emerge alive. During his poignant conversation with his mother, Thetis, ⟨. . .⟩, she says to him: "Ah me, my child, why reared I thee, cursed in my motherhood? Would thou hadst been left tearless and griefless amid the ships, seeing *thy lot is very brief and endureth no long while;* but *now art thou made short-lived* alike and lamentable beyond all men; in an evil hour I bore thee in our halls." (*Iliad* I, 13. Italics mine.) We note how Thetis acknowledges that Achilles is "lamentable beyond all men" because of the injury done to him.

As a prince of the heroic age, trained to be a leader of men in battle, to win honor in war was Achilles' whole *raison d'être*. That his death was imminent, and that he knew it, made the acknowledgment of his prowess all the more important to him. A hero would not attempt to escape his destiny by avoiding battle; that is why Achilles did not carry out his threat—nor did he ever intend to—to board his ship and sail for home. He withdraws from the battlefield in anger but remains in his camp. He knows that he will eventually return to the fight and fulfil his destiny. But he is all the more maddened by Agamemnon's insolence because the time left to him is brief. When death comes, he wishes it to come with the full honors due to the great hero he is. Thus, when this wild young man retires to his headquarters, he is in the grip not of one, but of two major emotions: wrath and frustration. It is necessary to realize his state in estimating the character of Achilles.

—André Michalopoulos, *Homer* (New York: Twayne, 1966), pp. 72–74

Charles Rowan Beye on the Looseness of Structure of the *Iliad*

[Charles Rowan Beye (b. 1930) is a professor of classics at Boston University. He has written *Ancient Greek Literature and Society* (1975) and *Ancient Epic Poetry: Homer, Apollonius, Virgil* (1993). In this extract, Beye explores the episodic structure of the *Iliad* and attributes this looseness to the poem's origin in oral tradition.]

The *Iliad* sometimes seems to have developed like churned butter, bits and pieces sticking together until a perceptible amount, clearly butter and no longer cream, clings to the paddle. By simple accretion, new words and phrases came which explained or defined more fully what had gone before. In this sense over fifteen thousand lines become spontaneous and natural amplification and redefinition of the poem's initial word "wrath." This theory of composition does not necessarily require a poet with a strong sense of unity; certainly the *Iliad* does not have a tight plot. Its episodic quality has concerned scholars whose critical standards are derived from well constructed novels that do not admit such extraordinarily loose narrative. These scholars are at pains to account for improprieties like Achilles' absence from the second through the eighth book. Perhaps, actually, various episodes in the *Iliad* are random happenings and do not depend upon each other, while the intellectual mind animated by an instinct for order, insisting upon cause and effect moves the critic to seek patterns and connections in even the smallest places. The problem is somewhat analogous to the nineteenth-century art critic who understands and accepts the exact representation of trees in the background of Italian primitive paintings (scaled naturally for perspective) but who cannot accept the convention of the French Impressionists who turn these trees into blobs of color, shadow, and light. The latter technique is far more realistic because it brings out the truly blurred and synthetic view of distant objects which humans have. In the same way the sometimes unsubstantial linkage between events in Homer's narrative represents more honestly the generally inexplicable train of human affairs. Nonetheless each element of the story clearly has value for the poet; he has introduced everything with consideration, sometimes to tell a story, sometimes to comment upon that story, and even at times to offer alternatives. The story nevertheless always remains. ⟨. . .⟩

The plot's looseness no doubt stems from the essentially ephemeral nature of oral poetry. The poet did add line to line. Beyond this, however, the story seems to show considerable organization that must have been the result of his having worked out a story line quite independently of creating the poem. Much of the story, of course, must have been traditional, which the poet simply took over, for it can be found elsewhere. Perhaps Homer acquired it in a simpler, more straightforward form, that is, the general and the hero quarrel, after which the hero retires until in "the nick of time" when almost all is lost he returns to the fight and dies gloriously—whereupon he is given a grand funeral. This plot with typical American modifications dominated C movies of the thirties. In our version the star fullback falls out with the coach, comes back to the game and wins, whereupon he and the girl fall in love at the school prom that evening. It is an important folk plot, but Homer has used it with sophistication. This plot turns on the psychological states of anger, rejection, fury, and acceptance; this psychodrama, as it were, is built upon the rhythm of the conventional plot although its elements are divided between the actions of Achilles and Patroklos.

Aristotle said that a story must have a beginning, a middle, and an end; the plot of the *Iliad* shows this. I should say that the books through the tenth are the beginning; from the eleventh through the seventeenth, the middle; and the last seven books, the end. Incidentally, originally there was no division into books. The poem was continuous, but capable of some kind of division by episode. Probably the Alexandrian scholars decided to divide the work into as many books as the Greek alphabet had characters (twenty-four) to identify them. The division attempts to follow the natural rhythm of the episodes. The beginning and end of a day are natural moments of pause and often book divisions occur there. There are, however, no *real* divisions. Occasionally episodes begin toward the end of one book and continue straight into the next. For example, when Achilles proceeds to arm himself at the end of the

nineteenth book (349*ff*) we have really the prelude to the battle in the twentieth book. One has to guard against the instinct to think in terms of chapters, intermissions, and the like, at these points. The action of the *Iliad* is absolutely continuous.
—Charles Rowan Beye, *The* Iliad, *the* Odyssey, *and the Epic Tradition* (Garden City, NY: Anchor Books, 1966), pp. 111–12, 114–15

W. F. Jackson Knight on the Appeal of Homer's Epic Poetry

[W. F. Jackson Knight (1895–1964) was an important classical scholar and translator. Among his publications are *Poetic Inspiration: An Approach to Vergil* (1946) and *Roman Vergil* (1971). He also translated Vergil's *Aeneid* (1956). In this extract from a posthumously published work, *Many-Minded Homer* (1968), Knight reflects on what has made Homer so pleasurable to read for generation after generation.]

Pleasure may not be the best thing to be got out of poetry, and it may not be the purpose for which poetry ought to be created. But there is no doubt that Homeric poetry was meant to give pleasure and did give pleasure; or that it can give keen pleasure still.

There are however plenty of different ways in which poetry can give pleasure, and it is a mistake to expect single poems to give pleasure in only one way. It would be a particularly bad mistake with Homer.

Perhaps Greek epic lays were originally performed to please the actual chiefs whose deeds they celebrated. That is likely, and the minstrelsy mentioned in Homer, the minstrelsy of Achilles, Demodocus and Phemius, might suggest that a keen personal interest could be taken by audiences in the heroes of the poem. A great motive of action for Homer's heroes is the desire to 'become a song for men yet to be'. Epic poetry carried personal fame, and almost certainly gave pleasure by satisfying the pride of heroes who were represented, and of their relatives, friends, descendants, and compatriots.

That after the earlier stages of epic this was one of the main sources of pleasure is much less likely. Homer's poetry almost all the time sacrifices advertisement to art. Like the Anglo-Saxon poem *Beowulf* which was imported into England and greatly enjoyed by audiences in no way connected with the characters, Homer was liked by Greeks independently of their peculiar interest in heroes related to themselves. ⟨. . .⟩

The joy of the *Iliad,* then, is not, and never was, just pride in the praise of ancestors, or great compatriots, for the praise is always subordinated by Homer to universal poetic truth; for the characters are universal, drawn without favour or fear. Nor, indeed, is it any one kind of joy only.

First there is the grand scheme of the whole poem to enjoy, and especially the recognition of the power of goodness at the end, how some law of god stands sure, in spite of battle-horror and Achilles' brutal, irresistible will; not quite irresistible, though, for a mother's love and its soft power are stronger, and Achilles becomes again at the last his own divine mother's son once more. We like finding that the ruthless, shameless tyranny of might does not have the last word, and that it prevails only for a time. There is an excitement, part ethical, part vindictive, in watching the process developing through suspense and delays. We like looking back from the end, and seeing how all of it has grown out of its beginnings, by unsuspected necessities, and the ready intervention of unknown powers at each turn.

But the victory of gentleness does not come quite as a surprise, for gentleness is never long forgotten. All the way, it balances in part the rough fear and pain and grief, at first overbalanced, and then overbalancing in the end; and it is there in two ways, in the home life, precarious in Troy, contrasted with the war, and in the similes of peace and nature, giving momentary relief, and reminders, amidst the fighting.

Yet there is a joy in the fighting itself, a savage thrill at casting restraint of fear and pity away, and letting go, the kind of

joy we had as children in reading adventure stories, and which the Greeks, younger as a race than we are now, must have enjoyed more than we when they were individually grown up. And there is too the more respectable thrill of danger, and of escape delayed that comes at last, with its relief and rest.
—W. F. Jackson Knight, *Many-Minded Homer: An Introduction* (London: Allen & Unwin, 1968), pp. 155, 157–58

JAMES M. REDFIELD ON HECTOR AND ACHILLES

[James M. Redfield (b. 1935), a professor of classics at the University of Chicago, is the author of *Nature and Culture in the* Iliad (1975), from which the following extract is taken. Here, Redfield explores the character of Hector by contrasting him with Achilles.]

Achilles' greatness is a greatness of force and of negation. He is different from other men by his greater capacity to deny, to refuse, to kill, and to face death. He is a heroic rather than demonic figure because his negations are founded not on perversity of will but on clarity of intellect. Achilles' wrath originates and continues because he can see exactly what Agamemnon is and exactly what his proffered gifts really mean. Achilles pursues his revenge so grandly and so far—even beyond Hector's death—because he knows exactly how inadequate revenge must be to the suffering which provokes it. Throughout the poem Achilles fully enacts his condition as he, with peculiar clarity, conceives it. We shall find this same clarity, and this same absorption in immediacy, in the reconciliation which ends the poem. Achilles' absolute incapacity for illusion makes him throughout the poem an insoluble problem to others and to himself. At the end, as I read him, the poet presents this insolubility to us.

Hector, by contrast, is a hero of illusions; he is finally trapped between a failed illusion and his own incapacity for disillusionment. Hector is surely a figure less grand than Achilles, but it is

Hector's story that gives Achilles' story meaning; Hector affirms all that Achilles denies. Treated in isolation, Achilles would be a mere existential cipher or borderline psychotic. Achilles achieves greatness only when we set him against the rich, functioning society of the Homeric world and see his tormented negations as, after all, a correct analysis of the contradictory internal logic of that world. Achilles brings destruction, first on Greeks and then on Trojans, because they have left him no choice. The source of his action is in their world; through the other characters, and particularly through Hector, we inhabit that world, and we see what problem it is that Achilles cannot solve.

It is also true that the poem would not move us if Achilles destroyed nothing of value to ourselves. Through Hector's story we come to see the wrath of Achilles as an event which has consequences for people like ourselves. Achilles is a strange, magical figure, with his immortal armor, his talking horses, and his sea-nymph mother, through whom his will has power even among the gods; Hector is a human creature, with wife and child, parents and brothers, friends and fellow citizens. Achilles' acts are always true to his shifting visions of himself; Hector has placed his life at the service of others. Between Hector and Achilles the outcome is never in doubt, for Achilles is superhuman, while Hector is only the sort of hero that we ourselves, at our moments of greatest aspiration, might hope to be. Through Hector's story, thus, Achilles is given a location in the human world. In the story of Hector Achilles appears as an emblem of those terrible facts men like ourselves can actually encounter. In Hector's story we see that, at the moment of such an encounter, wisdom and courage are not enough, that human strength and even human virtue can reach the limits of their efficacy.

The stories of Hector and Achilles are curiously discontinuous. They do not know each other. Achilles kills Hector, despoils and then later releases his body, not because Achilles hates Hector or forgives him but because in this way Achilles works out an action internal to himself. Hector's death is a debt owed by Achilles to Patroclus; Achilles releases Hector's body because at a certain moment Achilles is brought to see that Hector's death is not different from his own.

For Hector, on the other hand, Achilles is an unassimilable figure. He cannot be ignored, cannot be avoided, cannot be defeated, cannot even, at the end, be confronted with dignity. Throughout the story Achilles remains to Hector a riddle, an uncomprehended force. Between these two heroes there is a kind of vacant space at the center of the *Iliad*. This vacancy, at the end, the poet reveals to us.

Achilles is the great hero of the *Iliad,* and the *Iliad* is the story of the death of a hero; but Achilles does not die in the *Iliad*. The death of Achilles—or rather, his mortality—is a ruling fatality of the *Iliad,* but the pathos of the poem is concentrated in the death of Hector. The first line of the poem, as everyone remembers, is:

> The wrath, sing, goddess, of Peleus' son Achilles . . . (I.I)

We should also remember the last line:

> . . . so they completed the burial of horse-taming Hector.
> (XXIV.804)

In the account which follows we shall consider the story of the *Iliad* first as a kind of story, then as the story of what happens to Hector—in life, in death, and in the healing of death by the funeral.
—James M. Redfield, *Nature and Culture in the* Iliad: *The Tragedy of Hector* (Chicago: University of Chicago Press, 1975), pp. 27–29

William G. Thalmann on the Death of Achilles and the Epic Cycle

[William G. Thalmann (b. 1947), a professor of classics at the University of Southern California, has written *Dramatic Art in Aeschylus'* Seven Against Thebes (1978) and *Conventions of Form and Thought in Early*

Greek Epic Poetry (1984), from which the following extract is taken. Here, Thalmann examines the significance of Achilles' death in the *Iliad* and its mention in two other ancient sources.]

Epic accounts of Achilles' death are known from two sources: the last book of the *Odyssey* (xxiv.36–92) and Proklos's summary of the *Aithiopis,* one of the poems of the Epic Cycle. It appears that the story recapitulated the whole series of deaths in the *Iliad* that was discussed above. Nestor's son Antilokhos—like Patroklos, a special comrade of Achilles—was slain like him by the warrior who was then the main champion on the Trojan side, Memnon. Memnon, in turn, combines the features of both Sarpedon (Trojan ally, son of a divinity) and Hektor (his death at Achilles' hands was evidently preceded by a weighing of fates, with the divine mother of each hero begging for her son's life). In several ways Achilles' own death repeated that of Patroklos. He was slain by Apollo and Paris while attacking the city, and similarly Patroklos assaulted the Trojan wall, was driven back by Apollo, and was killed by the same god in conjunction with two mortals. As with Patroklos, there was a prolonged battle over Achilles' corpse until the Greeks finally carried it off the field. His funeral was celebrated with elaborate games, for which Thetis offered lavish prizes according to one version. Thetis, like Zeus and Ares forced to accept the death of her mortal son, mourned him with her sister Nereids and the Muses.

The accounts of the major heroes' deaths within the *Iliad* contain some specific anticipations of these events, which reinforce the general similarities. The dying Hektor's prophecy of the way Achilles will fall at the hands of Paris and Apollo in the Skaian gate (XXII.359–60) stresses the resemblance which that event will bear to Patroklos's death. When Apollo warns Patroklos to withdraw from the city wall, he indirectly foretells the death of Achilles: "It is not fated that the city of the greathearted Trojans be sacked by your spear, or by Achilles, who is much greater than you" (XVI.707–9). After Hektor's death, Thetis mourns her son's approaching doom (XXIV.83–86), much as the women of Hector's household lamented him while he still lived (VI.500–502). This is, however, a brief repetition of another scene as well. Hearing from her cave in the depths of the sea Achilles' lament for Patroklos, Thetis cries out and her sisters surround her (XVIII.35–64). They beat their breasts, and "Thetis led off the lament" (Θετις δ' εξηρχε γοοιο, l. 51); the same formula introduces speeches of mourning for Hektor later on (XXII.430, XXIV.747, 761). In tears, Thetis and her sisters then emerge from the sea and go to Achilles (XVIII.65–72). Thetis takes her son's head in her hands, in the same stylized gesture of mourning that Andromakhe will make with Hektor (XXIV.724). Surely in this scene Thetis and her sisters enact in advance their uncanny emergence from the sea to mourn the dead Achilles that so frightened the other Greeks and that was described in both the *Aithiopis* and the *Odyssey*.

On the basis of the remarkable similarities between the Iliadic and the non-Iliadic episodes, scholars have argued either that the *Aithiopis* influenced the *Iliad* or vice versa. But the question of influence and of the relative dates of the two poems is not very important. If the *Aithiopis* was the earlier, the *Iliad* was alluding to a poem that the audience probably knew. If the chronology was the reverse, the audience surely would have known the story of Achilles' death from epic versions that found their way eventually into the *Aithiopis* and the *Odyssey*. Our argument is unaffected whichever alternative is true. More probably, however, literary influence is not at issue here (and anyway the question cannot now be resolved). We seem to be dealing with a number of generic themes connected with the killing of a major hero that were used piecemeal in several scenes of the *Iliad* and were brought together most completely in the epic story of Achilles' death reflected in our sources. But it is precisely their typicality that makes them intelligible and enables the poet to put them to such profoundly expressive use, to deploy them in a sequence that clearly demands completion, so that the truly climactic death can overshadow the last six books of the poem without needing to be narrated directly or foretold circumstantially. The *Iliad* derives wonderful effects from the resonances that run through it from the whole mass of other poems that must have been in the air, and with the death of Achilles the poet plays on his audience's associations most movingly. He gives us the feeling of fate. Because it can be known in advance, the death is fixed and inevitable. Just as important as the simple fact of anticipation, however, is the sequence that events are to follow, which is prescribed by tradition but—for that very reason—significant. Against the background of the other heroes' deaths that are its forerunners, Achilles' death takes on coherence. That it must conform to a set pattern makes us sense a grimly beautiful order in events that is the shape of Necessity itself. Under these conditions, even the best of men is fallible, mortal, and doomed.

    These deaths are finally all the same. Each hero, as he kills and is killed, advances a process and falls victim to it. These men reach the height of human greatness in acts that turn out to be self-destructive.
>—William G. Thalmann, *Conventions of Form and Thought in Early Greek Epic Poetry* (Baltimore: Johns Hopkins University Press, 1984), pp. 49–51

PAOLO VIVANTE ON HECTOR'S CHARACTER

> [Paolo Vivante (b. 1921) is a professor of classics at McGill University in Montreal, Canada. He is the author of *The Epithets in Homer: A Study in Poetic Values* (1982) and *The* Iliad: *Action as Poetry* (1990). In this extract from *Homer* (1985), Vivante studies the character of Hector as exhibited in his actions.]

Hector is the most human of the heroes in the *Iliad.* One obvious reason is that we see him at home, in close relation with his family and people. This, however, is not my point. It would be utterly inadequate to say that Hector is a typical husband, father, son, and soldier, for none of these roles is taken for granted. They are caught at their delicate points of realization; and these points converge, summoning up a comprehensive image. Each instance tells us what it is to be a man in any of these concurring and blending capacities.

    As a result, Hector appears quite removed from the mythical background. In book 6 of the *Iliad,* for instance, he is as natural as anyone could be. We might, then, expect him to behave like any modern character endowed with definite likes and dislikes, idiosyncrasies, and other realistic traits. But this is obviously not so. Why not? Because the heroic may be humanized, but not converted into anything willful or whimsical. Homer only deals with basic conditions of life; and equally basic are his characters, inseparable as they are from the instances which bring them into being. Hector thus solely exists and lives through the action intrinsic to him. It would not do to see him behaving at random, being fastidious or morose or titillated by anything in particular. No, the full moment of experience absorbs him entirely, even if it is resolved in the lightness of a smile or a passing gesture: action or state of being rather than behavior. Within the brief succession of days that see Hector alive, there is no room for asides or extemporizing to bring out any supernumerary trait.

The integration of character and action is here carried to an extreme. Hector is made self-evident step after step. No particular attitude of his should be attributed to predetermined characteristics or to external motives. Why, for instance, his love for Helen (cp. *Il.* 24.762, 6.360)? Fondness, inclination? A chivalrous temperament? The reason lies, rather, in the fact itself. Helen's beauty is no arbitrary matter. She is a shining presence; the spell she casts, as well as its attending woe, are established in the ways of nature and fate. And it is not for Hector to sit in judgment. He has heard her cry (*Il.* 6.344ff.), as he has Andromache's. Being so imaginatively responsive, how could he not sympathize with her plight? One might say, at any rate, that the baffling truth of human relations strikes corresponding chords in himself.

The mystery of character is thus entwined with that of events. Again, why, we may ask, does Hector rebuke Paris so sharply only to be reconciled with him a little later (cp. *Il.* 3.76, 6.521ff., 13.788)? Or why is he so stung and yet sobered by the reproaches of Sarpedon and Glaucus (cp. *Il.* 5.493, 17.170ff.)? Or why is he so impatient with Polydamas only to regret it at the last moment (*Il.* 22.100)? Levity or recklessness? No, here is versatility, which on each occasion comes to terms with the truth of things; here is malleability and freedom of spirit. For we know how strains of character spontaneously arise from the brunt of experience, how events test and shape

a man's temper when he fully meets their challenge and tastes life to the core.
—Paolo Vivante, *Homer* (New Haven: Yale University Press, 1985), pp. 54–56

M. M. WILLCOCK ON IDOMENEUS

[M. M. Willcock (b. 1925) is a professor of classics at the University of Lancaster in England. He is the author of *A Commentary on Homer's* Iliad (1970) and *A Companion to the* Iliad (1976). In this extract, Willcock comments on the place of Idomeneus in the *Iliad*.]

Idomeneus is an important figure in the *Iliad*. The Cretans appear to be Achaeans who live in Cnossos and the other cities which used to be the centre of Minoan civilisation. Idomeneus is described as grandson of Minos, but he is certainly a Greek. The tradition has blurred history, and knows nothing of the destruction of the Minoan palaces. In the *Iliad* Idomeneus is not only a major Achaean leader like any other, but he has the third largest contingent in the army, providing no fewer than eighty ships with their complement of troops. He is distinguished as an efficient and experienced fighter, and (uniquely) as middle-aged and grey-haired. He did some pretty good work in Book XIII, when the Greeks were under heavy pressure, his appearance there following a semi-comic scene between him and his second-in-command Meriones behind the lines (XIII. 240–97).

Meriones is always portrayed as an active lieutenant, a second-rank commander, but with his own distinguishing features, particularly that he is efficient, keen, and has a tendency to aim low. The scene I referred to in XIII came about because neither Meriones nor Idomeneus knew that the other was not at the front, and when they met behind the lines each was a little embarrassed about what the other might be thinking. The scene shows a most natural humanity; and it is memorable that they came back into battle together on foot (XIII.304–5), not on chariots, Meriones consulting his superior as to where along the line they should join in.

Idomeneus then did pretty well for a time, killing distinguished Trojans and allies: Othryoneus who had been a suitor for Cassandra, Asius the leader of the Trojan attack on the wall in XII, Alcathous Aeneas' brother-in-law, and Oenomaus, one of Asius' lieutenants. But Idomeneus got tired, not being as young as he used to be, and withdrew in good order (XIII.512–16).

Whether we speak of 'foreshadowing' or of 'composition by theme', that scene in XIII should be in our minds now as we are hearing the events in XVII. There are close similarities. Idomeneus is an able fighter—he actually hits Hector—; but he is no longer a young man, and needs some protection. Meriones treats him with suitable deference.

In the gruelling fight for Patroclus' corpse Idomeneus is in some danger. The Greeks are starting to fly. It appears that Coeranus, observing the danger, has brought up the chariot, looking to the safety, not of his immediate officer, but of the senior commander. And Coeranus pays for this brave act with his life. Charioteers were vulnerable when they were doing their duty. The classic example is the charioteer of Polydamas (XV.445–53). They had to keep the chariot close to the front, offering a means of escape to the fighter they served; and it was not easy to protect themselves, because they were occupied with the horses and the reins. ⟨Bernard⟩ Fenik finds five examples in the epic of charioteers killed by weapons aimed at their *paraibatai*. After the death of Coeranus, Meriones bent down, picked up the reins, gave them to the older man, and said 'Get back to the ships'.

A little *vignette*, then, of responsible and disciplined behaviour of soldiers in the front line. Homer knew about war. The president of the Classical Association in England in 1971 was General Sir John Hackett, who had been a commander under General Montgomery in the desert fighting in the last war. This general gave his Presidential Address that year, and in it he drew attention to extraordinarily similar attitudes, particularly among ordinary soldiers, in the *Iliad* and in his experiences in the army. He has an interesting paragraph in which he speaks of the qualities needed for the functional efficiency of a fighting group, including behaviour so practiced that it becomes routine, leaving little scope for imagination or fear. Homer seems to be characteristically sympathetic to the ethos of the army. He understood these things, as indeed Napoleon said; Virgil did not.

Let us hear the commentators. Leaf, author of the main library edition of the *Iliad* in English, an outstandingly good Homerist of course, but with strong analytical tendencies, was attracted by the suggestion, which he says originated with Bentley, and was again proposed by Düntzer, to change Μηριονao in 610 to 'Ιδομενηος, with a hiatus-deflecting γε before it, thus at a stroke removing the problem about the chariot which Idomeneus mounted. German scholars had favoured this, or other emendation, apart from those who simply deleted the whole passage as a late interpolation. Von der Mühll merely comments that Idomeneus' effort at resistance to Hector falls flat, and Hector kills "einen Kreter aus Lyktos". All of this shows to my mind the unacceptable face of traditional analysis, the search for weakness and inconsistency blinding the scholars to the clear human implications of the lines.

Worse still, Fenik has a dangerous lapse of memory here. He describes the end of our scene as follows: "At this point Meriones needs no further convincing. He seizes the reins and beats a hasty retreat with Idomeneus to the ships." Now that is too bad! Meriones does not withdraw, but stays and plays a full part in the continuing battle. He merely gets Idomeneus out of danger. Nor is Fenik the only scholar to make that mistake. It was made before by the admirable Albracht: "Schleunigst greift nun Meriones aus dem Wagen heraus die zu Boden gefallenen Zügel auf, 620, und beide enteilen zu den Schiffen"; and it will no doubt be repeated in the future because of the influence of Fenik's book. Thus the credit for Meriones' self-denying act, just like the credit for Coeranus' perception of his duty, is lost through superficial and careless comment.

Homer does not say, of course, that Coeranus brought up Meriones' chariot expressly to save Idomeneus, because he saw that as his immediate task; or even perhaps because Meriones so instructed him. We have to understand it. It is

71

after all the obvious meaning of the lines. And Homer, as the ancient critics said, sometimes leaves us to understand things κατὰ τὸ σιωπώμενον, without expressly saying them. Alternatively, this may be an abbreviated version of something that had been told more explicitly in the past. It is a feeling that we sometimes have in the *Iliad,* and more so in the *Odyssey,* that the tale has been told before, probably many times, and some of the detail has been condensed. Not that the poet intends to condense, but he is so used to the story that he omits some of the explanation. The *Iliad* is not an instantaneous, single creation. It is evident that there have been tellings of the tale before. I do not personally mind that sort of argument, provided we add that the previous tellings were by the same poet. We may reasonably see the *Iliad* as the culmination, the high point, of the art of a long-experienced oral bard.
—M. M. Willcock, "The Final Scenes of *Iliad* XVII," *Homer: Beyond Oral Poetry: Recent Trends in Homeric Interpretation,* ed. J. M. Bremer, I. J. F. DeJong, and J. Kalff (Amsterdam: B. R. Gruner, 1987), pp. 187–89

Mark W. Edwards on Ancient Greek Folktales and the *Iliad*

[Mark W. Edwards, a professor of classics at Stanford University, is coauthor of *The* Iliad: *A Commentary* (1985–93) and the author of *Homer: Poet of the* Iliad (1987), from which the following extract is taken. Here, Edwards discusses Homer's use of ancient Greek folktales in the *Iliad.*]

It is obvious to anyone that the plots of the *Iliad* and the *Odyssey* share common features with other well-known tales; it is easy to find striking parallels between Odysseus's adventures with villains, monsters, and beautiful females and those of Sindbad the Sailor, James Bond, or Captain James T. Kirk, and between Achilles' revenge for the killing of his best friend and the plot of many a western movie. The fact that the tales were already placed in the legendary past for Homer's audience gave them the remoteness that brings added appeal and makes the fantastic possible; modern fantasies like Tolkien's *Ring* tales also use the distant past for this purpose or, more commonly, the future, as in the science fiction and space fiction genres. Besides similarities in plot, small motifs with immediate appeal constantly recur in literature and life; Odysseus's journeying until he finds someone who mistakes the oar he carries for a winnowing fan *(Odyssey* II.119ff.) finds a parallel in the weary Yukon resident who longs to "tie a snow shovel to the hood of my car and drive south until nobody had the faintest idea what the damn thing was" (*San Francisco Chronicle,* 31 December 1982).

Modern scholarly analyses of the structure of folk tales have made it possible to identify common features in stories, and a good deal of work has also been done in comparing the parallels between the Homeric epics and other ancient Greek tales. In recent years we have also reached a better understanding of how Homer uses plot motifs in different ways and how he modifies the shape of myths, or even invents new ones, to suit his purpose. Structural analyses and comparisons of this kind not only offer the delights of taxonomy and theorizing, but assist our understanding of the poet's methods and can sometimes explain features of a plot or episode that have led to misapprehensions in the past.

The following discussion will deal first with large-scale structures of the plots of the two epics; then, by a rather arbitrary but practical division, with smaller-scale repeated motifs; and finally with the ways in which Homer can be seen to manipulate or invent the material of myth for his own purposes.

Perhaps the commonest of all basic story patterns is the absence or loss of a person or persons, the troubles that result, and the eventual return of the person or recovery of the loss and the ending of the problems. In more abstract terms, a state of order is thrown into disorder and eventually returned to order. This is generally called the "withdrawal, devastation, and return" pattern, or the "eternal return". This obviously forms the main plot of the *Odyssey*: the initial scenes in Ithaca show the evils resulting from Odysseus's absence, then the young son Telemachus sets off to find his father, and the eventual return of both brings about the punishment of the wicked and the end of the troubles.

The more detailed analysis of the elements of such a basic story, as described by Propp, appear even more clearly in the Circe episode in *Odyssey* 10.203ff. Odysseus is told that his men have been overcome by Circe (Propp's functions 8-8a) and sets out to find them (9-11), meets the divine helper Hermes (12-13), and is given the magical agent, the herb moly, which will make him immune to Circe's magical powers (14). He confronts Circe (15-16) and is touched by her wand (17), but defeats her (18) and recovers his men (19). He and Circe then go to bed together (31?), but this "marriage" of the hero, which appears in full form in the reunion of Odysseus and Penelope, is in the Circe episode more likely to be an adaptation of the motif of the fairy seductress who unmans or destroys her lovers, as do Ishtar (in *Gilgamesh*), Eve, la Belle Dame sans Merci, the Lorelei, and many others. Divine helpers with gifts, like Hermes here, also appear to rescue Menelaus when he is stranded off Egypt (Eidothea, who gives him not only counsel but also sealskins for disguise; *Odyssey* 4.435ff.) and Odysseus himself when he is shipwrecked by Poseidon (Leucothea, who gives him her garment for protection; *Odyssey* 5.351ff). The pattern recurs in the divinely made armor given by Hephaestus to Achilles, the gifts of Medea to Jason and Ariadne to Theseus in Greek legend, and of course in the marvelous devices given to James Bond in the opening scenes of his adventures and to Frodo in Tolkien's *Ring* cycle. The many other folk tale parallels in the *Odyssey* have been identified in the work of Woodhouse and Page.

The "withdrawal-devastation-return" structure is the obvious foundation of the *Iliad* plot, too, with revenge and consolation tales added at the end. In fact it is repeated several times in that poem, for besides Achilles' loss of Briseis, which is the motive for his withdrawal and the defeat of the Greeks, and the paradigm of Meleager that Phoenix relates, it is Agamemnon's loss of Chryseis that leads to the plague and begins the plot; and of course the loss of Helen is the reason for the entire Trojan War. This special form of the structure, the abduction of women and consequent troubles, is very common in myth—

Persephone, Ariadne, and Medea are famous instances—and its popular appeal shows up in Herodotus's account of the origin of the conflict of Greeks and Persians (I.I-5). He blames it on the successive abductions of Io by the Phoenicians and Europa and Medea by the Greeks, until Paris was inspired by the impunity of the offenders in these tales to steal a wife from Greece. Aristophanes' lighthearted account of the origins of the Peloponnesian War of his own time in successive reprisals for the abduction of whores by the Athenians and Megarians (*Archarnians* 523ff.) confirms the popular appeal of such tales.

Another familiar pattern in the plot of the *Iliad* is the loss of the hero's best friend, which is repeated later in the Trojan War cycle in the case of Antilochus, who is killed by Memnon and avenged by Achilles in the *Aethiopis* (*Odyssey* 4.187-88). It also appears in *Gilgamesh* (associated with the mortality of the hero himself, since it is as a result of Enkidu's death that he sets off to find the secret of everlasting life), in the David and Jonathan tale in *Samuel*, in the part of Oliver in the *Song of Roland*, and in the Greek myths of Castor and Pollux, Theseus and Pirithous.

The quarrel of Achilles and Agamemnon in *Iliad* 1 is also modelled on a standard pattern. There are references to a quarrel between Agamemnon and Menelaus (*Odyssey* 4.134-50), to one between Achilles and Odysseus (sung by Demodocus, *Odyssey* 8.73-80), to one between Ajax and Odysseus over the armor of Achilles (*Odyssey* 11.543ff.) and perhaps others lie behind the hints of Paris's resentment against the Trojans (6.326) and Aeneas's against Priam (13.459ff.).

Some of these patterns occurred in much the same form in other epics of the Trojan cycle. The clearest examples are the rescue of Nestor by Diomedes (8.80ff.), which is similar to the much more poignant rescue of the old man by his son Antilochus in the *Aethiopis*, in which the younger man lost his life to the hero Memnon; and the scene in which Diomedes is wounded in the foot by Paris (11.369ff.), which recalls the scene in the *Aethiopis* where Achilles himself is struck in the heel and killed by Paris. Such parallel scenes may well be examples of standard patterns of story, rather than proving a

dependence of one poem upon the other. But of course Homer, like other bards, must have known and sung a much wider range of songs than the *Iliad* and the *Odyssey*, and the influence of one song upon another must have been considerable.
—Mark W. Edwards, *Homer: Poet of the* Iliad (Baltimore: Johns Hopkins University Press, 1987), pp. 61–64

Katherine Callan King on Common Motifs in the *Iliad*

[Katherine Callan King (b. 1942), a professor of classics and comparative literature at the University of California at Los Angeles, is the author of *Achilles: Paradigms of the War Hero from Homer to the Middle Ages* (1987), from which the following extract is taken. Here, King explores the major motifs of the *Iliad*, including Achilles' epithet as the "best of the Achaians," and their significance in the epic.]

In order to comprehend most clearly how later poets use Achillean motifs to animate their own heroes and political messages, it is necessary to have a thorough understanding of how these motifs function in the Iliadic portrait, which became archetypal because of Homer's great authority. My task in this chapter will therefore be to set forth these motifs—many of which for centuries had the power instantly to evoke Achilles—and to discuss them in the context of Homer's conception of his hero.

Of prime importance is Achilles' undoubted claim to the epithet "best of the Achaians," an epithet that comprises not only physical qualities but also a humanistic complexity that survives, if fitfully, into the Italian Renaissance. My analysis of Homer's use of Achilles' superlativeness leads naturally—but subvertingly—into an examination of the unsurpassed prowess displayed in Achilles' rampage, a period of total and uncharacteristic brutality that became an important motif of Euripides, Catullus, and Vergil as well as for Renaissance poets. Achilles' murderous heroics in this rampage are carefully nuanced by analogical allusion and simile to remove any sense of human nobility from the warcraft that eventually kills Hektor and thus creates another important motif: the effective conquering of a city by wreaking personal vengeance on that city's champion.

There remains the question of why Homer so nuanced Achilles' fighting. The first part of my answer discusses how Achilles' unique combination of qualities and behaviors functions as part of Homer's critique of heroic society and his exploration of what it means to be human, mortal. The famous wrath and the equally famous honor and glory are the focal points of this section, which delineates Achilles' agonizing reassessment of the kind of glory he is willing to die for. The next part analyzes what becomes perhaps the most misrepresented motif in Achilles' career: the final reconciliation with Priam, which in Homer's version profoundly alters the reader's understanding of what it means to be both human and "best."

All the images, speeches, and scenes that create powerful motifs for later poets contribute in the *Iliad* to an original portrait that distinguishes Achilles as much for his self-awareness as for his wrath; as much for his need for meaningfulness as for his pride; as much for his compassion as for his ability to kill. All contribute to the poignancy of the last scene, which takes place under the shadow of Achilles' own imminent death. By prefiguring but not consummating this death within the *Iliad*, Homer leaves us with the eternal poignancy of certain death waiting within a superlative living mind and body; he leaves us, that is, with the essence of what it means to be mortal. But when in his later postwar epic Homer shows us Achilles dead, the poignancy of his predicament is gone. In the *Odyssey* it is Odysseus who engages our emotions; Achilles' character is simplified so as to set in clear relief the now more complexly developed portrait of the man who in many ways is his opposite. My final brief look at Achilles' role in the *Odyssey* will thus adumbrate the classical stereotyping of Achilles as a warrior of quick anger, stark honesty, superlative prowess and obsession with worldly honor.

—Katherine Callan King, *Achilles: Paradigms of the War Hero from Homer to the Middle Ages* (Berkeley: University of California, 1987), pp. 1–2

KEITH STANLEY ON THE SIGNIFICANCE OF THE *ILIAD*

[Keith Stanley (b. 1934) is an important classical scholar and author. He has written *The Shield of Homer* (1993), from which the following extract is taken. Here, Stanley argues that in the *Iliad* Homer established a unified literary epic that preserved the oral traditions of the ancient Greeks.]

There remains the perennial difficulty of recovering the Homeric in Homer: of isolating not so much a nucleus of material as the essential stamp left by an eighth-century singer on his inheritance. It has been argued that the price of Achilleus' withdrawal from battle—the death of Patroklos—is a Homeric addition to the story of the Wrath, and that the parallel development of the tragedy of Troy is his creation also. This impartiality toward opposing sides suggests the emergence of a remarkable creative sensibility from the limitations of tribal memory clinging to a glorified past to valorize the present: a sensibility so much a part of *Iliad* that it could reasonably be attributed to the essential "Homeric" stage of the poem. It is not axiomatic, however, that a poem presenting the Greeks' antagonists with such empathy would have met with panhellenic endorsement and popularity even (or perhaps especially) if their world were modeled on that of eighth-century Ionians. And it is worth asking how far an analysis of international conduct in terms of illusion—not simply the *ate* inflicted by Zeus on Agamemnon, but a characteristc inherent in a given political structure (in the case of the Trojans)—can be attributed to the eighth-century mind, however alerted to a sense of history it may have been by epic itself and by the discovery of the material world of its "heroes."

⟨. . .⟩ certain characters of our *Iliad* are likely to have been more critically drawn than were their originals. Patroklos and the personalities who dominate the scenes in Troy—Priam, Helen, Andromache—are necessary as they are to the basic parallelism within the Homeric *Iliad* and were perhaps not greatly altered by our poet. Most likely his, however, is the elaboration of the more extreme elements of excess in Achilleus—as displayed in Books 20 and 21 in particular—and the refinements upon the terms of his rejection of the Greeks in

1 and 9 and of his reinvolvement with them in 23. The parallel between the self-delusive Hektor and the humbled but uncomprehending Agamemnon may also be taken as a reflection of our poet's rethematizing impulse. In the case of Agamemnon, the original articulation of a conflict between the extraordinary individual and the flawed king had become, in so many terms, a political irrelevancy during the archaic period; but it is a conflict that might well have acquired the status of a moral paradigm during an era in which the brevity of power and position was demonstrated in case after case. The elements of "guilt culture" that we have noted in Books 9 and 23 provide an essential indication of the poet's view of the past, but this perspective seems unlikely for an early stage in the organization of an otherwise conservative tradition and may well represent a retrospective framework that emerged only in its latest phase. And although it may be, as antiquity believed (Herodotus 2.53), that Homer in some sense gave the Greeks their gods, it seems equally likely that our poet's particular gift was Zeus: a god not merely of force and wayward impulse but the Zeus of compassion, of respect for and commitment to the evolution of values human and divine in terms that parallel Achilleus' own revaluation of *time* by *philotes*.

Barring new evidence, the relationship between Homer and his forebears remains in many important respects uncertain and unknowable, except perhaps through hermeneutic methods that will change with our understanding of the poem and of ourselves. It is nevertheless clear that he rightly represented to his successors a new standard for the tradition he inherited and passed on. It should be equally clear that the poet of our *Iliad* is responsible not simply for an inestimable achievement in the preservation of a fund of traditional poetry, mixed in technique and function: He in fact accomplished the generic transformation we mentioned at the outset, establishing a precedent and shape for the unified literary epic of the classical tradition that has haunted all subsequent efforts at renewal with a just apprehension of obsolescence.

His work is marked, like its most noteworthy progeny, by traces of revision. For during the period of progressive reduction to writing, interpretation had become not simply an immediate, passive response to the familiar codes of oral epic but an active creative agent in the exploitation of latent potentialities in a developing text. To the temporal aspect of oral epic was gradually joined that of literary space and thus literary form, with extension and further fixation of meaning through the recoding devices we have seen in our poet's rearrangements, expansions, and recontextualizations of earlier material. Distanced from its inherited medium, the reference of the poem had moved—by anonymous steps appropriate to maintaining the authority of the tradition—from praise to analysis, from the tribal to the international, from the customary to the moral and to a vision, through the tragedy and failure of Achilleus and Priam, of ultimate gain. Our *Iliad* thus represents not the end of an oral tradition or the beginning of a literary one but stands, with its residue of inconcinnities, at the arbitrary end of a process of textualization marked by its adoption under regulation as a civic institution. The burden of interpretation then passed from poet—across a blinding hiatus—to exegete; and the text itself survives as not so much a patchwork or palimpsest as a commentary on purpose and accident, with corresponding hazards, frustrations, and rewards: where "everything is negligible, yet everything counts."

—Keith Stanley, *The Shield of Homer: Narrative Structure in the Iliad* (Princeton University Press, 1993), pp. 293, 295–96

Graham Zanker on Achilles and Priam

[Graham Zanker (b. 1947) is the author of *Realism in Alexandrian Poetry* (1987) and *The Heart of Achilles* (1994), from which the following extract is taken. Here, Zanker explores the significance of Achilles' behavior with Priam.]

In plotting Achilles' course, my chief concern has been to question the precise ways in which Achilles' behavior with Priam goes beyond the demands of conventional social institutions and the respect and pity that he showed with Eëtion but that characters like Hekabe and Apollo doubt he is capable of any more. The salient factors are identified and discussed more fully in the preceding chapter. First, though he accepts the ritual importance of *tîmê* and gifts to both his duty to Patroklos and to his transaction with Priam, he shows a remarkable insouciance over acquiring honor and ransom-gifts, as is shown by his use of the gifts of cloth in which to wrap Hektor's corpse, and by his sneering sideswipe at Agamemnon, who will demand ransom for Priam if he learns of Priam's presence in Achilles' hut. Second, Achilles acts generously toward Priam without any hope of the future reciprocity that guest-friendship normally entails; both men know that Troy's wealth is spent and that the city is to fall soon, and Achilles knows anyway that he is soon to be killed. Third, he respects the behest of Zeus Hikesios in accepting Priam's supplication, offering him a meal, kind words, and a bed, but he seems to go beyond Zeus' requirements by having the corpse washed and anointed, by his gesture of lifting it onto its bier—thereby starting the funeral rites of Hektor—and by his offer of the eleven-day truce. Fourth, he proves significantly responsive to the personal aspect of Priam's appeal, especially to the invocation of his relationship to Peleus, and he shows that he has recognized the value of human relations, which he is prepared to foster precisely at the moment when he knows for certain of his imminent death, and which he is ready to express through his admiration for Priam, by calling him "old man, my friend," and by clasping Priam's right wrist to reassure him that he has nothing to fear (671-72). Fifth, he is accorded Zeus' novel *kûdos* by his own moral choice to give back Hektor's corpse. Sixth, his generosity to Priam outstrips his respect for Eëtion, noble though that is within its more standard framework.

How shall we characterize Achilles' behavior toward Priam as he reverts to and surpasses the generosity he used to show before his conflict with Agamemnon, pinpointing the compelling existence of nonselfish drives? The word that I wish to propose is *magnanimity,* which has already, quite naturally crept into the discussion. I must therefore define what I mean by magnanimity and show how Achilles displays the quality, even though there is no word in Homeric Greek to describe it. I shall then examine whether Greek philosophical discussion of magnanimity and related responses, especially those of Plato and Aristotle, offer any retrospective insight into the gratuitous benevolence of Achilles, and where it stands in relation to Greek society and thought. Finally, I shall try to examine the uniqueness of Achilles' moment of magnanimity in early Greek epic. I suggest that in this respect also Homer earns the title of "the first teacher and way-finder of the tragedians" given him by Sokrates in the *Republic* (595c1f.).

I hope to have demonstrated in this book that in the meeting between Priam and Achilles, a moment exists in the *Iliad* in which we can discern a character acting in a kind way toward another, who is moreover an enemy, without any dominating sense of self-interest, motivated instead principally by a feeling of common humanity in the face of common mortality. Parallels can be drawn from modern times—for example, from the trench warfare of World War I. S. Weintraub describes the spontaneous truces on the Western front, which "were most likely to occur in bad weather, and men emerging from flooded trenches often were not shot at by the other side even when orders to fire were in effect." Otherwise, we have the incident on the first day of the Battle of the Somme, when "German stretcher-bearers came out at certain points, under white flags, and picked up British wounded near their own wire," and the occasions on which soldiers strayed near enemy lines, in foggy conditions, for example, and were merely told to go back by the sentries, who could not bring themselves to shoot an exposed enemy. *Magnanimity* seems the most natural word to describe such behavior. The dictionary defines the quality as "Nobility of feeling; superiority to petty resentment or jealousy; generous disregard of injuries," but such a description does not seem to do justice to the extent of the generosity involved in the ancient and modern examples we have before us, where the rifts between the two sets of parties are anything other than "petty," and where the motivation to disregard the rifts is, each in its own way, of a highly complex kind. Nor will we find appropriate to our inquiry the sense of the haughty superiority suggested by the dictionary's definition, whereby, for example, a general might spare the lives of a few defeated troops on the grounds that he was far too grand to bother to attend to the execution of a few more paltry, insignificant souls. Such "magnanimity" is closer to disdain. Moreover, we tend nowadays to

consider magnanimity to be the greater where the element of self-interest in the motivation is small. We are accustomed to assigning different degrees of moral status to different acts of magnanimity, and few of us would seriously demand an absolute, Kantian purity of motive from altruism, of which magnanimity is an aspect. Most of us, though we might distantly admire it, would more likely be repelled by the severity of Kant's example of the man whose natural sensitivity for others' suffering has been displaced by some personal grief of his own, but who nonetheless, despite the cessation of his naturally kind inclinations, does a beneficent act, purely out of a sense of duty that a beneficent act must be done, at which point alone, according to Kant, his action has genuine moral worth. We would react even more strongly in the case of the man whose natural endurance and fortitude make him expect the same qualities in other people, so that he is cold and indifferent to others' suffering, and who, though he acts benevolently not from inclination but from pure duty, wins a higher moral worth than a man of a good-natured temperament.
   —Graham Zanker, *The Heart of Achilles: Characterization and Personal Ethics in the* Iliad (Ann Arbor: University of Michigan Press, 1994), pp. 127–30

Works by Homer

Greek text:

Opera. Ed. Demetrios Chalkokondyles. 1489.

Ilias. Ed. Aldo Manuzio. 1504.

[*Works.*] Ed. Jacobus Micyllus and Joachim Camerarius. 1541.

Opera. Ed. Samuel Clarke. 1729–40. 4 vols.

[*Works.*] Ed. Thomas Grenville, Richard Porson, et al. 1800. 4 vols. in 2.

[*Works.*] Ed. Wilhelm Dindorf. 1824–28. 3 vols. in 2.

Ilias. Ed. Karl Friedrich Ameis and Karl Hentze. 1882–87. 2 vols. in 8.

The Iliad. Ed. Walter Leaf. 1886–88. 2 vols.

Opera. Ed. David B. Monro and Thomas W. Allen. 1902–12. 5 vols.

The Iliad. Ed. A. T. Murray. 1924–25. 2 vols. (with English translation).

Iliade. Ed. Paul Mazon et al. 1937–38. 4 vols.

Iliad. Ed. M. M. Willcock. 1978–84. 2 vols.

Iliade. Ed. Maria Grazia Ciani. 1990.

English translations:

The Iliads of Homer. 1611.

The Whole Works of Homer. Tr. George Chapman. 1616.

Homer His Iliads. Tr. John Ogilby. 1660.

Homers Iliads in English. Tr. Thomas Hobbes. 1676.

The Iliad of Homer. Tr. Alexander Pope. 1715–20. 6 vols.

The Iliad of Homer. Tr. James Macpherson. 1773. 2 vols.

The Iliad and Odyssey of Homer. Tr. William Cowper. 1791. 2 vols.

The Iliad. Tr. Edward, Earl of Derby. 1864. 2 vols.

The Iliad. Tr. William Cullen Bryant. 1870.

The Iliad of Homer. Tr. Andrew Lang, Walter Leaf, and Ernest Myers. 1883.

The Iliad of Homer. Tr. Samuel Butler. 1898.

The Story of Achilles. Tr. W. H. D. Rouse. 1938.

The Iliad. Tr. E. V. Rieu. 1950.

The Iliad. Tr. Richmond Lattimore. 1951.

The Iliad. Tr. Martin Hammond. 1987.

The Iliad. Tr. Robert Fagles. 1990.

Works about Homer and the *Iliad*

Bloom, Harold, ed. *Homer's* The Iliad. New York: Chelsea House, 1987.

Bowra, C. M. *Homer.* New York: Scribner's, 1972.

Camps, W. A. *An Introduction to Homer.* Oxford: Clarendon Press, 1980.

Carpenter, Rhys. *Folktale, Fiction and Saga in the Homeric Epics.* Berkeley: University of California Press, 1946.

Carter, Jane B., and Sarah P. Morris, ed. *The Ages of Homer.* Austin: University of Texas Press, 1995.

Chadwick, H. Munro. *The Homeric Age.* Cambridge: Cambridge University Press, 1967.

Crotty, Kevin. *The Poetics of Supplication: Homer's* Iliad *and* Odyssey. Ithaca, NY: Cornell University Press, 1994.

Dietrich, B. C. *Death, Fate and the Gods.* London: Athlone Press, 1965.

Else, G. E. *Homer and the Homeric Problem.* Cincinnati: University of Cincinnati Press, 1965.

Fenik, Bernard, ed. *Homer: Tradition and Invention.* Leiden: E. J. Brill, 1978.

Ford, Andrew. *Homer: The Poetry of the Past.* Ithaca, NY: Cornell University Press, 1992.

Griffin, Jasper. *Homer on Life and Death.* Oxford: Clarendon Press, 1980.

Harrison, E. L. "Notes on Homeric Psychology." *Phoenix* 14 (1960): 63–80.

Higbie, Carolyn. *Measure to Music: Enjambement and Sentence Structure in the* Iliad. Oxford: Clarendon Press, 1990.

Hogan, James C. *A Guide to the* Iliad. Garden City, NY: Anchor Books, 1979.

Janko, Richard. *Homer, Hesiod, and the Hymns: Diachronic Development in Epic Diction.* Cambridge: Cambridge University Press, 1982.

Jensen, Minna Skafte. *The Homeric Question and the Oral-Formulaic Theory.* Copenhagen: Museum Tusculanum Press, 1980.

Kirk, G. S. *Homer and the Oral Tradition.* Cambridge: Cambridge University Press, 1978.

———. *The* Iliad: *A Commentary.* Cambridge: Cambridge University Press, 1985–93. 6 vols.

———. *The Language and Background of Homer.* Cambridge: Cambridge University Press, 1964.

———. *The Songs of Homer.* Cambridge: Cambridge University Press, 1962.

Leaf, Walter. *Homer and History.* London: Macmillan, 1915.

Lord, A. B. *The Singer of Tales.* Cambridge, MA: Harvard University Press, 1960.

Luce, J. V. *Homer and the Heroic Age.* London: Thames & Hudson, 1975.

Lynn-George, Michael. *Epos: Word, Narrative and the* Iliad. Atlantic Highlands, NJ: Humanities Press, 1988.

MacCary, W. Thomas. *Childlike Achilles: Ontogeny and Phylogeny in the* Iliad. New York: Columbia University Press, 1982.

Martin, Richard P. *The Language of Heroes: Speech and Performance in the* Iliad. Ithaca, NY: Cornell University Press, 1989.

Mireaux, Emile. *Daily Life in the Time of Homer.* Tr. Iris Sells. New York: Macmillan, 1965.

Mueller, Martin. *The Iliad.* London: Allen & Unwin, 1984.

Murray, Gilbert. *The Rise of Greek Epic.* 4th ed. London: Oxford University Press, 1934.

O'Brien, Joan V. *The Transformation of Hera: A Study of Ritual, Hero, and the Goddess in the* Iliad. Savage, MD: Rowman & Littlefield, 1993.

Otto, Walter F. *The Homeric Gods.* Tr. Moses Hadas. New York: Pantheon, 1954.

Page, D. L. *History and the Homeric* Iliad. Berkeley: University of California Press, 1959.

Parry, Milman. *The Making of Homeric Verse.* Oxford: Oxford University Press, 1971.

Pratt, Louise H. *Lying and Poetry from Homer to Pindar.* Ann Arbor: University of Michigan Press, 1993.

Pucci, Pietro. *Odysseus Polutropos: Intertextual Readings in the Odyssey and the* Iliad. Ithaca, NY: Cornell University Press, 1987.

Rubino, Carl A., and Cynthia W. Shelmerdine, ed. *Approaches to Homer.* Austin: University of Texas Press, 1983.

Schein, Seth L. *The Mortal Hero: An Introduction to Homer's* Iliad. Berkeley: University of California Press, 1984.

Scully, Stephen. *Homer and the Sacred City.* Ithaca, NY: Cornell University Press, 1990.

Seaford, Richard. *Reciprocity and Ritual: Homer and Tragedy in the Developing City-State.* Oxford: Clarendon Press, 1994.

Segal, Charles. *The Theme of the Mutilation of the Corpse in the* Iliad. *Mnemosyne* suppl. 17. Leiden: E. J. Brill, 1971.

Seidel, Michael, and Edward Mendelson, ed. *Homer to Brecht: The European Epic and Dramatic Traditions.* New Haven: Yale University Press, 1977.

Shive, David M. *Naming Achilles.* New York: Oxford University Press, 1987.

Simpson, R. Hope. *The Catalogue of the Ships in Homer's* Iliad. Oxford: Clarendon Press, 1970.

Slatkin, Laura M. *The Power of Thetis: Allusion and Interpretation in the* Iliad. Berkeley: University of California Press, 1991.

Sullivan, Shirley Darcus. *Psychological Activity in Homer: A Study of* Phren. Ottawa: Carleton University Press, 1988.

Taplin, Oliver. *Homeric Soundings: The Shaping of the* Iliad. Oxford: Clarendon Press, 1992.

Thornton, Agathe. *Homer's* Iliad: *Its Composition and the Motif of Supplication.* Göttingen: Vandenhoeck & Ruprecht, 1984.

Vivante, Paolo. *The Homeric Imagination.* Bloomington: Indiana University Press, 1970.

———. *The* Iliad: *Action as Poetry.* Boston: Twayne, 1990.

Webster, T. B. L. *From Mycenae to Homer.* 2nd ed. London: Methuen, 1964.

Wofford, Susanne Lindgren. *The Chance of Achilles: The Ideology of Figure in the Epic.* Stanford: Stanford University Press, 1992.

Wolf, F. A. *Prolegomena to Homer.* Tr. Anthony Grafton, Glenn W. Most, and James E. G. Zetzel. Princeton: Princeton University Press, 1985.

Yamagata, Naoko. *Homeric Mortality.* Leiden: E. J. Brill, 1994.

Index of Themes and Ideas

ACHILLES: his death and the epic cycle, 64–67; and Hector, 62–63; and Priam, 80–83; and his role in the poem, 11, 12, 15, 16, 17, 19, 21, 22, 23, 24, 25, 26–27, 28, 29, 30, 31, 32, 37, 38, 41, 42, 43, 44, 52, 55, 56, 57, 58, 59, 60, 61, 72, 74, 75, 76, 77, 78, 80; and his wrath, 39–40

AENEAS, and his role in the poem, 14, 19, 25, 31, 75

AESCHYLUS, compared to Homer, 49

AGAMEMNON, and his role in the poem, 11, 12, 14, 15, 16, 17, 18, 20, 24, 30, 37, 38, 40, 42, 47, 49, 56, 62, 74, 75, 78, 79, 81

AIAS, and his role in the poem, 15, 16, 18–19, 21, 22, 23, 30, 38, 44, 75

ANDROMACHE, and her role in the poem, 15, 27, 29, 31, 34, 39, 40, 41, 66, 68, 78

APHRODITE, and her role in the poem, 11, 13, 14, 20, 25, 26, 32, 45, 46, 47

APOLLO, and his role in the poem, 11, 12, 14, 15, 16, 18, 21, 22, 25, 26, 27, 28, 31, 33, 65, 80

ARES, and his role in the poem, 14, 19, 21, 25, 26, 32, 65

ATHENA, and her role in the poem, 11, 14, 15, 16, 17, 18, 21, 23, 25, 26, 27, 30, 31, 32, 56

BEOWULF, and how it compares, 61

DEIPHOBOS, and his role in the poem, 27, 31

DIOMEDES, and his role in the poem, 14, 15, 17, 18, 20, 30, 32, 38, 40, 75

GILGAMESH, and how it compares, 75

HECTOR: and Achilles, 62–64; and his character, 67–69; and his role in the poem, 11, 13, 15, 16, 17, 18, 19, 20, 21, 22, 23, 25, 26, 28, 29, 30, 31, 32, 37, 38, 39, 40, 41, 43, 44, 49, 64, 65, 66, 70, 77, 79, 81

HEKABE, and her role in the poem, 15, 26, 27, 28, 29, 31, 40, 80

HELEN, and her role in the poem, 11, 13, 14, 15, 16, 26, 29, 31, 39, 40, 41, 42, 45–47, 68, 74, 78

HEPHAISTOS, and his role in the poem, 23, 24, 25, 26, 32, 38, 74

HERA, and her role in the poem, 11, 12, 14, 16, 17, 20, 21, 23, 24, 25, 26, 31, 32, 40

HERMES, and his role in the poem, 25, 28, 74

HERODOTUS, compared to Homer, 75, 79

HESIOD, compared to Homer, 42, 44

HOMER: and the appeal of his epic poetry, 60–62; and the heroic, 40–45; and his imagination, 34–36; life of, 7–10; and his skill at word painting, 33–34

IDOMENEUS, and his role in the poem, 19, 69–72

ILIAD, THE: and ancient Greek folktales, 72–76; the heroic elements in, 55–58; the historical basis of, 47–50; common motifs in, 76–77; the origins of, 53–55; the significance of, 78–80; the structure of, 50–52; the looseness of structure of, 58–60; the structural and thematic integrity of, 36–39; thematic and structural analysis of, 11–29

KARENINA, ANNA (*ANNA KARENINA,* Tolstoy), as compared to Helen, 45–46

LORD OF THE RING, THE (Tolkien), and how it compares, 73, 74

MENELAUS, and his role in the poem, 11, 13, 14, 15, 16, 17, 18, 20, 22, 23, 30, 31, 45, 75

MILTON, JOHN, compared to Homer, 36

NESTOR, and his role in the poem, 11, 12, 15, 16, 17, 19, 20, 30, 40, 65, 75

NIETZSCHE, FRIEDRICH, compared to Homer, 46

ODYSSEUS, and his role in the poem, 17, 20, 24, 30, 40, 46, 52, 72, 73, 74, 75, 77

ODYSSEY, THE, and how it compares, 52, 53, 65, 66, 72–74, 76, 77

PARIS, and his role in the poem, 11, 12, 14, 15, 16, 18, 19, 20, 27, 31, 40, 45, 65, 68, 75

PATROKLOS, and his role in the poem, 17, 19, 21, 22, 23, 24, 27, 28, 30, 31, 37, 38, 49, 52, 63, 65, 66, 70, 72, 78, 81

POSEIDON, and his role in the poem, 16, 19, 20, 21, 25, 26, 32

POULYDAMAS, and his role in the poem, 20, 23, 31, 68, 70

PRIAM: and Achilles, 80–83; and his role in the poem, 13, 16, 26, 27, 28, 31, 32, 39, 40, 75, 77, 78

SARPEDON, and his role in the poem, 19, 21, 22, 31, 65, 68

SHAKESPEARE, WILLIAM, compared to Homer, 36, 44, 49–50

SONG OF ROLAND, and how it compares, 42, 75

THETIS, and her role in the poem, 12, 16, 23, 24, 28, 31, 32, 39, 52, 63, 65, 66

TOLSTOY, LEO, compared to Homer, 45–46, 47

VERGIL, compared to Homer, 34, 71

ZEUS, and his role in the poem, 12, 13, 14, 16, 17, 18, 19, 20, 21, 22, 23, 24, 25, 27, 28, 31, 32, 33, 39, 40, 52, 65, 78, 79, 81